Walk with Jesus

How to
Listen to and Follow Jesus
Every Day Everywhere

By
Chris Suitt

CMA X RESOURCES

You can't take yesterday's or tomorrow's steps toward Jesus today. You can only choose to walk with Him right now.

To Jesus, the God of the Universe,

Who wants to walk in relationship with me everywhere I go 24/7;

to my *Bible Impact* partners;

and to my family – Jan, Doug, and DeAnna –

for walking this journey with me.

Table of Contents

Introduction

It's Time for a Walk

Jesus doesn't need me to do anything for Him; He wants me to do everything with Him.

"My sheep listen to My voice; I know them, and they follow Me. I give them eternal life." (John 10:27-28a)

*D*id I actually hear what I thought I heard? "Go. Take your Bibles. Be quiet before Him and just listen to your God." This was a foreign concept to me at the time. Yet, right there in seminary, my professor was stopping class and telling us to go find a quiet place on campus and just listen to our God.

I'd been a believer in Jesus for 13 years at the time. I had never heard someone tell me to listen to God without limiting it to just the written Word of God. My teacher was asking us to try to hear the voice of God for ourselves. I picked up my backpack and went on a walk. It would become more than just a walk with my feet, but a walk with my heart as well. It would be the walk that started a journey; the first of many walks throughout the rest of my life.

Does My God Actually Want to Talk with Me?

Could it be true that the God of the universe, my Savior, actually wanted to talk with me? Does He care that much about a mere human? I went looking for a quiet place, free of distractions that would allow me to be still before my Jesus. I knew if I sat under a tree I would be distracted by all the visuals surrounding me – people walking by, clouds in the sky, ants in the grass, etc. My walk led me to one of the quietest places I knew – the campus chapel.

Once I found the perfect solitary place, I stretched out on the floor with my Bible in hand. I opened the source of truth that measures all of life's experiences, to begin a journey that has continued throughout my life.

I didn't hear an audible voice from heaven, though biblically this is possible.[1] Instead, I heard a soft voice inside me. I wasn't sure what to make of it at first. Yet this Voice spoke to me. This was the first time I ever realized that my God wanted to have a two-way conversation with a child of His!

I can't say that I was very good at hearing His voice from that point forward. If I had, it would have saved me a lot of heartache over the next ten years. Then again, it was that heartache that led me to search the Scriptures to see how the Spirit of God changes lives outside of a miracle. These life-changing principles became the basis for my book, *More Than a Sunday Faith*, about building and living with a biblical worldview. In that book I lay out the *Set Free Nowww* acronym as a way to remember some of the foundational biblical tools each believer should use in order to listen to and follow Jesus every day everywhere in community (John 10:27).

These principles are the tools that enable a believer to screen out all the other voices vying for their attention so they can zero in on just one – their Savior's voice. I've used these principles over the last 16 years to better help me hear from my Jesus and follow Him throughout my day.

A Journey to Hear God's Voice

It is this journey of learning to hear God's voice that has led me into a deeper relationship with Him. This is what *Walk with Jesus* is all about. I needed the *Set Free Nowww* principles to show me how God changes a life so I could stay in His presence everywhere I went. These principles also showed me that walking in the presence of a very personal God is a central theme of Scripture, from Genesis to Revelation.

This journey started with a walk at seminary, a place where I never thought I would be challenged in that way. Up to that point in my life, I loved my God, but the only way I knew how to express that love was obedience. The problem was that this obedience was primarily an outward conformity, not a change that came from the inside (Romans 12:2). I had learned and lived by the motto, "It is better to burn out for God than rust out." Eventually

I came to see that both sides of that statement were wrong!

The truth is that Jesus doesn't need me to do anything *for Him*. He wants me to do everything *with Him*. As God, He is self-sufficient; He lacks nothing. He doesn't need anything from me to make Himself complete. Period. In my years as a pastor, I used to think it was my job to make disciples for Christ. In Scripture, however, we see that God can accomplish that in His own way and in His own timing.[2] God does choose, though, to use believers in bringing people to Himself. He commands us to disciple them to follow Him everywhere they walk in life (Matthew 28:18-20). Does God *need* us? No, but He does want to use us.

No Burn Out or Rust Out Required

How could I avoid burning out *or* rusting out for Jesus? My breakthrough came at a conference for church planters, where a pastor/speaker shared something that further revolutionized my walk with God.

He mentioned at one point that he had a three-hour staff meeting with his boss every Monday. I was puzzled. He was the senior pastor! Who, then, was his boss? Calmly, he went on to explain that, according to 1 Peter 5:1-4, he was simply a shepherd serving under the Chief Shepherd, Jesus Christ. Therefore, he needed to meet with his *Boss* on a regular basis. It was his *Boss* who said, "I will build My church." Building the church was Jesus' responsibility, not the pastor's. Instead, it was this pastor's job, as a shepherd serving Jesus, to discover how his Boss wanted His sheep to be shepherded. Having a weekly "staff meeting" was a simple way to do this.

It took me a few years to even start putting this into my schedule, and then a few more years to learn how to make it actually work for me. What I didn't mention earlier is that, during my seminary listening experience, I ended up falling asleep on that chapel floor! I guess I should have stayed outside after all; the chapel was too quiet! Unfortunately, it was the same when I finally got around to having my weekly "staff meetings." I would try to find a quiet place to hear Jesus, but, no matter where I went, I would eventually end up falling asleep.

The Journey Continues: Prayer Walks

I tried having these meetings in the morning, in the afternoon, or at night when I'm usually at my best. Nothing worked, until I started to walk while I prayed. There were vast amounts of open land behind my house where I lived, and I could walk for a good three to five miles. I started my staff meeting by heading for the hills, literally. I exited my front door, turned left and walked straight into wide fields and rolling hills. While they were an unattractive brown most of the year, I'm not complaining; it was there that I really learned how to listen to my Lord. It was on these long walks that I learned how to hear Him and then to stay in His presence afterward, whether at work, at home, or anywhere else.

Over the years, I've experienced silence, as well as heated conversations with my Boss. Some of these prayer walks have been nothing special, while others got me excited for the days ahead. These walks have taken me into various places throughout the country and world and have taught me many valuable lessons on walking with Jesus.

Walk with Jesus will hopefully help you discover that your journey on this planet has less to do with a destination – heaven – than it does with a person – Jesus. A healthy walk with Jesus depends upon Him speaking to you directly *and* through His Word. This is vital if you want to live the abundant life He promised to bring you.

The Whys of Walking in His Presence

More Than a Sunday Faith gives you the tools to replace your worn-out character with His eternal character (see Appendix I for a cliff note version of these tools). Armed with Christ-like character, you have the ability to come into and stay in the presence of God. *Walk with Jesus* is about the reasons for and the benefits of walking every day everywhere in His presence.

I'm inviting you to take a walk with me. It's the kind of walk that will take you beyond *going* to church to *being* the church everywhere you go. It's a walk of living in His presence as you practice picking up and using your biblical tools in the Spirit's power. It's about hearing Jesus' voice and following Him. It's not about just living in the hope of heaven some day. It's a personal walk that is not about getting rewards later, but enjoying them and your God now.

Everything we're looking for in life is found in the presence of our God, but somehow we still choose to turn our back on Him and live our own way! From the beginning of human history, people have been running from the presence of God (Genesis 3:8). This running continues with believers in Christ today, but not to their benefit. Paul explains in Galatians 5:1 that those who place their faith in Jesus can be set free from sin and its consequences, such as shame, guilt, emptiness, loneliness, insecurity, insignificance, and eternal separation from Jesus (see John 8:31-32). God welcomes believers into His presence, but it's our choice whether we stay there or not.

Jesus Asks Us to Walk with Him

Jesus is not demanding to manage our time or thoughts so that He can stuff more activities into our schedules. He's not asking us to burn out for Him. No, He's asking us to walk in His presence as we allow His Spirit to shape our daily schedules. Sometimes He has left my to-do list as it was when I left the house that morning. Other times, He has changed the order, or removed some items while leaving others for the next day or week. The point is, I don't have to do anything for Him to make Him or myself feel better. I do what I do each day to be with Him. This book is about your love for Jesus and your walk with Him, who, by the way, modeled this kind of lifestyle for us. He never did anything *for His Father*; everything He did, He did *with His Father*.

Our God is asking the same of us: *do everything we do with Him, rather than for Him*. In John 21:15-17, it fascinates me how Jesus talked to Peter, who had recently denied three times that he even knew Jesus. In building Peter back up, Jesus asked Peter, "Do you love Me?" He didn't say, "Peter, get on with the job. Go make disciples." Jesus started with love, not with expectations. He asked Peter, "Do you even like Me, let alone love Me?"

Life with Jesus was not supposed to be about what Peter could do *for* Jesus. It was supposed to be about what Peter could do *with* Jesus. Jesus knew Peter was shying away from Him because he had messed up big time. So Jesus started by asking Peter, as He does with us, "Do you love Me? If so, then follow Me."[3] I believe Jesus' heart to Peter and to us is expressed in the song, *Where You Go I'll Go*.

Where You go I go
What You say I say
What You pray I pray

Jesus only did what He saw You do
He would only say what He heard You speak
He would only move when He felt You lead
Following Your heart following Your Spirit

How could I expect to walk without You
When every move that Jesus made was in surrender
I will not begin to live without You
For You alone are worthy and You are always good[4]

Take the Next Step: Want to Walk

This is the type of walk that I hope you'll join me on through the following chapters. Are you ready? Any journey begins with the desire to take the first step in a particular direction. You're being asked to do what I was asked to do, "Be quiet and listen to your God." So ask yourself, "Do I want to walk in the presence of my God?" "Do I want to hear God's voice?" "Am I open to the idea that my God wants to have two-way thoughtful conversations with me?"

Let's talk as we walk together.

Chapter 1

You Can Live in His Presence

Is your way working for you?

"Therefore, brothers, since we have confidence to enter the Most Holy Place by the blood of Jesus, by a new and living way opened for us through the curtain, that is, His body...let us draw near to God." (Hebrews 10:19-22a)

"What are you doing?" Jesus would often ask me on my prayer walks. "Are you walking with Me or just getting some exercise on your own? Are you walking to walk or to listen to Me?"

For me, the scenery isn't normally a distraction from walking with God. In fact, it's often through the scenery that I've felt His presence. I see white-tailed jackrabbits scurrying along their trails. I hear birds softly tweeting to each other as they hide in the short shrubs along the path or on the electric wires above. I see owls on wooden fence posts turn their heads an apparent 360 degrees to keep their eyes on me. No, I cause my own distractions; I'm the one stopping myself from making the most of my walks.

Walking Keeps Me Close to Him

I love walking with my God. It's through prayer walking that I've learned to stay close to Him. And it's my prayer walks that God uses to show me how to stay in His presence throughout my day...not simply when I need guidance on sensitive issues or insight on what He wants me to say to His people through a Sunday message. These walks have taken me many places – from grassy, rolling hills to golden-ripened wheat fields; from vegetable farmlands to tracts of houses with their black asphalt roads. I've walked flatland paths that were straight and wide as well as climbing paths that were steep and narrow, and through the familiar fields around my house to hills and valleys where I'd never been before.

In order to help me keep track of where I'm going, I've put an app on my smart phone. It not only lets me know my exact location at any given moment, but it also keeps track of my pace. Knowing how fast I'm going is a blessing and challenge at the same time. You'll rarely be able to accuse me of going too slow, but it's pretty hard to feel the presence of my God when my heart is beating right out of my chest.

I've also discovered over the years that I can cover greater distances in less time as my stamina has improved. This is not a bad thing, unless it takes away from listening. I can get so focused on setting a faster pace that I forget why I'm walking in the first place. It's not for exercise, though that's a definite benefit. My heart rate is good for a man my age, but that is not why I *prayer* walk. I have to remind myself that it's supposed to be a time where I'm experiencing Jesus' presence, not a race or a challenge to cover more territory. No, I prayer walk because I want to practice walking with my God, the source of everything I want in life. These prayer walks are even more necessary when I need to hear what He has to say about daily events or struggles I'm facing.

The point of taking these walks is to be close to Jesus. It is Jesus who said, "I am the way, the truth and *the life*." All that humanity is looking for – love, security, satisfaction and significance – is found by walking with Him. The question remains, "Will I walk every day everywhere, in His presence?" A personal walk in the presence of God has always been what our God has wanted from us. Again, He doesn't need me to do anything *for Him*. He simply wants me to do everything *with Him*. I believe you can find this message from one end of Scripture to the other: God wants us to walk in His presence.

In the Beginning, God Walked

We find mankind in the presence of God from the very outset of the Word of God. He talks with Adam and Eve in Genesis 1:27. He physically puts Adam in the garden and shows him how to live in Genesis 2. Then, for the first time in Scripture, we find the Lord walking with mankind in Genesis 3.

What's interesting about the context is that God is walking with them because Adam and Eve were trying to *hide* from "the presence of God" (Genesis 3:8 KJV). Adam and Eve were always in the presence of God. The question became, "Would they recognize Him as even being there?" I believe the answer is found in Psalm 139:7 where it says, "Where can I go from Your Spirit? Where can I flee from Your presence?" The word "go" is the same Hebrew word for walk. The Hebrew word for presence, *panim*, in both passages can be translated as "face," "in the face of," or "turning your face." Thus, though Adam and Eve couldn't ever leave the presence of God, they were attempting to ignore God by turning their faces away from Him to avoid looking at Him.

There's a game that parents play with a newborn child. They look over their baby's basinet with a smiling face. Suddenly, one parent puts their hands over their face and says, "Where'd you go? Where'd you go?" Then they take their hands away with a smile on their face while saying, "There you are!" All the while their child is cooing in delight. Did anyone actually go anywhere? No. The child is still securely in the presence of their parents. The same thing happened with Adam and Eve, except it was no child's game. Essentially, they became the first agnostics when they ignored God, and it brought catastrophic consequences.

Adam and Eve were created to walk in the presence of their God. It was only *after* they turned their back on God through direct disobedience that shame overwhelmed them to the point they scurried to the trees to hide!

Yet God went after them. He literally walked in the garden *with* them, which emphasized His love *for* them. I believe He was trying to reestablish a face-to-face connection. They had turned their faces from and then their backs on Him as they walked off. By "walking" with them, maybe He could let them look into His eyes and see how He felt. Yes, they had messed up, but He still loved them, and wanted to reestablish His presence in their lives!

A Sweet Walk in the Presence of God

This is God's desire for us all – to personally walk in His presence. He wants us to choose to acknowledge that He is there, and to stay focused on being in His presence. We see a beautiful example of this the next time the phrase "walk with God" is used with a human, a few chapters later in the Bible. Genesis 5:24 states that Enoch walked with God. What's interesting with Enoch is that their relationship was so close that God said, "Come on home!" before Enoch physically died!

It appears that this unique walk didn't start until after the birth of Methuselah, Enoch's firstborn son. The Bible states, "*After* he became the father of Methuselah, Enoch walked with God," (Genesis 5:24, emphasis added). I smile when I read this verse, thinking, "Leave it to having children to straighten out any human being!" I can empathize with Enoch. I love being a parent, but there are definitely times when I've had to rely extra hard on Jesus. Children can challenge you in ways you never thought possible!

Who knows what Methuselah did, or what life after Methuselah brought, but Enoch acknowledged and focused on the presence of God for 300 years! Enoch had other sons and daughters in this time as well; he didn't seclude himself on some mountain to think about God. No, he walked with God in everyday life, despite the challenges that came with being a dad. His personal walk in the presence of his God was so wonderful that God took Enoch home to be with Him, where any barriers between them would fall away.

One Person's Walk Saved the World!

The next major character in Scripture also walked in the presence of God was Noah. He is famous for how he built the boat and saved humanity from total annihilation (you can read about it in Genesis 6-9). Let's look at Noah's life before he built the ark and gathered the animals.

By this time in history, humanity had turned their backs on God's presence and was in active rebellion against Him…except for one man, Noah. He "was a righteous man, blameless among the people of his time and he walked with God." (Genesis 6:10) Noah didn't live in a vacuum. He had a family. He had a job. He also had tremendous peer pressure to stop walking in the presence of his God. The entire world was literally circling the drain!

Because of his walking in the presence of God, God could trust Noah with a super-human task – the salvation of the human race. Noah's walk took him totally out of his comfort zone. Noah wasn't a general contractor. He was a "man of the soil." He grew grapes and made wine (Genesis 9:20), but Noah was soon to learn a lot about animal tending as well. And what did Noah do? He listened to and followed where God took him, even into the crazy adventure of building a huge boat, collecting hordes of animals and food to feed them and his family as well! He must have figured his God would show him what to do with each step he took, which is exactly what happened.

Noah built a boat while he walked with his God. He prepared food for the coming animals while being with his God. He told people to get right with God while working hard on his construction project (2 Peter 2:5). We don't stop living our daily lives in order to walk with our God. No, we walk in the presence of our God every day everywhere. We do this by using our biblical tools to listen to and follow Jesus.[1]

A Face-to-Face Encounter with God

The walking saga continues with Abraham, the next major biblical character. He was challenged by God "to walk before Me" (Genesis 17:1). The Hebrew word translated here as "before" is the same word translated as "face" with Adam and Eve. In Abraham's context, it meant for him to keep his face turned toward God. In other words, Abraham was to walk in the presence of his God. What a wild walk that was! He moved from his hometown to a new country, and went from being childless to having children when well past his prime. All this and more took place because Abraham chose to live in the presence of his God... which his son Isaac and grandson Jacob did as well.[2]

This Presence Comes in Physical Form – The Tabernacle

This walking in the presence of God took on a slight twist with the next scriptural characters – Moses and the nation of Israel. Moses quotes the Lord in Leviticus 26:11-12 as saying to the nation, "I will put My dwelling place among you, and I will not abhor you. I will *walk among you* and be your God, and you will be My people." It was this Lord who brought them out of slavery into freedom. It was this Lord who wanted a personal walk with His people. It was this Lord who wanted His people to live in His presence every day everywhere.

This is one of the reasons the Lord gave Moses very specific construction plans for the building He would "live in" – a tent called the Tabernacle (Exodus 25:8). Of course, even the universe is too small to hold our great God. Nonetheless, this tent made of earthly material with human hands was going to house the Creator of the universe to show His people they could walk in His presence, just like their forefathers Abraham, Noah, Enoch, and Adam and Eve. Once this Tabernacle was constructed, God came and "lived" in it (Exodus 40:34-37). It was so full of His glory that even Moses could not enter it at first.

Through the Tabernacle, God was able to walk with *an entire group of people*. We see in Numbers 9:15-23 that a cloud covered the Tabernacle by day and what looked like a cloud of fire covered it by night. When this cloud moved, the nation was to pull up their tent stakes and move with it. When the cloud stopped, they were to set up camp. If the cloud stayed, the people were to stay. If the cloud moved, they were to move. They were to follow this Tabernacle, the presence of God, everywhere it went and whenever it went.[3]

The people had a choice, however. When God walked, they could either stay where they were, or walk with Him. They could either choose to listen and follow, or to close their ears and not follow. If He moved and they didn't, they "left" His presence and would have to deal with the consequences of that choice.

What's fascinating is the fact that the Lord created a system for reconciliation for *if* His people chose to turn their backs on Him. All the various offerings found in Leviticus chapters 1-7 relate to coming back into and staying in the presence of God.[4] Even the Hebrew word for sacrifice, *corban*, means "to draw close." The Lord wanted so much for the Israelites to live and walk with Him that He provided a way for constant connection.

God Wants to Walk with His People

This desire continues into the second half of the Bible as well. John 1:14 states, "The Word became flesh and made His dwelling among us." Does this sound similar to what you've read so far? Jesus, the Living Word, became flesh or "tabernacled" Himself so God could live with us. John is making a direct correlation between the earthly tabernacle made by humans to Jesus taking on an earthly tent (made partly by a human – Mary).

It was this Jesus who said in John 8:58 that He is the "I AM," the same phrase used when God identified Himself to Moses. After Jesus made this statement, the Jewish leadership knew exactly what He was saying – that He was God, and the very same God who spoke to Moses and walked with the Patriarchs. There was no way this man Jesus, who was born to Mary, could be old enough to have been around in Moses' day, let alone in Abraham's.[5] Not surprisingly, Jesus' listeners didn't believe Him, and were even ready to stone Him to death for blasphemy.

The idea of people walking in the presence of God is a theme throughout Scripture. Jesus simply put an exclamation point on it. The God who created the universe wants His creation to personally walk with Him every day everywhere, and Jesus came to show us that it could actually be done!

Because Jesus became human, He could die in order to defeat our adversary the devil, and death (Hebrews 2:14-18). Because of what Jesus did, we can live each day looking into the very eyes of God; we don't have to wait until we get to heaven (Hebrews 4:14-16). Because of what Jesus does, we can personally have a face-to-face relationship with our God every day everywhere (Hebrews 10:19-23).

God Already Lives in You

Paul writes in 2 Corinthians 6:16, "We are the *temple of the living God*. As God has said: 'I will live with them and *walk among* them, and I will be their God, and they will be My people,'" (emphasis added).

God is not living in a tabernacle today. He is living *inside* His people, those who have put their faith in Jesus as Lord and Savior. He is living inside a tent made of earthly materials, just like He did inside the Israelite Tabernacle, and later the Temple. God has been walking with His followers from the beginning of time. Why would He stop now? Believers in Jesus can be like Adam, Eve, Enoch and Noah; we can imitate Abraham who walked with the Lord who appeared to him. As believers in Christ, we have the presence of God inside us. Believers can follow the Lord, just like the Israelites followed the cloud, because we have the Spirit living inside us to guide us each step of the way (Galatians 5:25).

From one end of the Book to the other, Scripture shows living-and-breathing people walking in the presence of the Lord. This is what our God wants from us; not a Sunday only faith, but a real faith that works in every situation. Through His death and resurrection, Jesus gives us the ability to stay in the presence of

God 24/7. We can draw near to God in full assurance that He wants us there (James 4:8).

Take the Next Step – It's Your Choice

You were designed to live in God's presence, but it's your choice whether you'll start that journey. Will you focus on the distance you have yet to travel in life, and/or on the pace, or will you focus on Jesus? Will you cram your schedule full of things to do, or will you commit yourself to living in God's presence throughout your day? Will you look into the loving face of Jesus or face the world? It's your choice.

If you choose to focus on the world, don't forget to *often* ask yourself, "Does this work for me? Is it bringing me what I'm looking for in life?" If not, it may be time to choose to walk with God and to live each day using biblical tools (Appendix I).

David wrote in Psalm 27:4-5, "One thing I ask of the LORD, this is what I seek: that I may dwell in the house of the LORD *all the days of my life*, to gaze upon the beauty of the LORD and to seek Him in His holy temple." His heart's longing was to live where his God lived right now, not when he died. His daily focus was on his God. Be like David. Turn your face to Jesus and stay focused on Him. *You were created to walk in His presence.*

The golden-ripened wheat fields along a walk near my house.

Chapter 2

Your God is
the Source of All Good Things

The bigger your view of God is, the smaller your challenges become.

"Praise the LORD. He determines the number of the stars and calls them each by name. Great is our God and mighty in power, His understanding has no limit." (Psalm 147:1a,4-5)

*W*ow. *This feels weird and peaceful at the same time!* I was on a prayer walk right after a certain truth impacted my life. What was that truth? God is full of mercy and full of grace *at the same time* (Psalm 116:5). It may be a surprise that these two traits are found in the first half of the Bible (i.e. the Old Testament, or Tenach) as well as in the second (i.e. the New Testament). Our God is the same yesterday and today, as He will be tomorrow. He never changes. He can be trusted.

So why was this prayer walk any different from the other good ones I had taken? It was different because I had just sinned, taken my drug of choice (see Appendix I). And yet, I was out prayer walking. This would have been impossible for me before I learned the *Set Free Nowww* principles. I used to feel that if I messed up I had to punish myself before I could get up and start walking in the presence of my God again. I believed that I deserved to be punished for what I'd done, and had to stay in my shame-filled state for a little while. There was simply no way I felt I could get up and walk again so soon.

Corrected Vision

I knew about God's grace and mercy. I believed in them both. I simply had a distorted view of how they applied to me. Truth: I deserved to be punished for taking my "drug of choice" or sinning. Truth: Jesus took my punishment and His blood covered my sin – biblical mercy. Truth: I didn't deserve to be helped up to walk again. Truth: Jesus extended His nail-scarred hands to pull me up so I could get back into the presence of my God. This is what Scripture calls grace.

I can't tell you why it took so long for those truths to transform my life, but I'm glad they did. Because of Jesus, not me, I had forgiveness. Because of Jesus, not me, I could start walking in the presence of my God again. Why stay down in that pit of guilt and shame?

Let me be completely transparent, there are times when I purposefully take my drug of choice and there are times I don't. Like we saw last chapter, however, God provided the way for me to draw near to Him again through the sacrificial system, which was completely fulfilled in what Jesus did on the cross and in rising from the tomb. Our God doesn't like it when we sin, and it doesn't make our lives any better, either. But this is why He sent Jesus to redeem us.

That day, the truth that God is full of grace and mercy finally sunk into my brain. I could finally take His hand and start walking with Him sooner than I had ever done before in my life. It felt awkward at first, but over time I came to enjoy being able to immediately return to walking with my God, leaving the guilt behind.

A Small Insight into Your God

There is simply no way anyone would want a personal walk in the presence of God if they didn't think He was good and that following Him would make their lives better. If you think He's mad at you, why would you even want to come into His presence? We might believe in Him so we could get into heaven, but there would be no real relationship along the way to getting there. *Until we see Jesus is the source of everything that we need, we won't trust Him enough to live in His presence.* How we view God will determine how much of our day, let alone our life, we will spend with Him. So, what is *your* God like?

The Bible, as powerful as it is, can't begin to cover all of who our God is. He is far too vast and eternal to describe in one book. This is why we'll need an eternity to get to know Him. The Bible does teach us what God is like, though, so that's a good place to start in following Him.

Know Your God, Not About Your God

First and foremost, God is love (Jeremiah 31:3; John 4:16). The verb is crucial here. He *is* love; this is who He is at the very core of His being. He would stop being God if He ever stopped loving. This is a huge truth to focus on. It meets one of the three basic needs of every human being – the need to be loved. Your God, the most powerful person in the universe, says He loves you and wants you to walk in His presence. What does that say about how important you must be to Him?

He might love me, but that doesn't mean He really wants to be around me. I already know too many people like that, we may think. Yes, humans may fail, but God never does. He says He will never leave you (Matthew 28:20). What part of "never" gives you room to believe He will abandon you (Hebrews 13:5)? There is no place in this universe, let alone on this planet, that you could ever go to get away from the presence of God (Psalm 139:7-12).

He loved you before you loved Him, or ever did anything that made you worthy of being loved. He placed such high value on you that He sent Jesus to die for you. How much more valuable can you get than God dying for you to show you His love? If He loved you before you had the power to do anything right, what makes you think He will stop loving you if you do something wrong? *But I'm not good enough for Him to help me. I'm just a* _____. It might surprise you to know that Jesus treats everyone the same (Romans 2:11). Your God holds you in His hands, knows everything you have done or ever will do, looks you straight in the eye, and says, "I love you!" Who else knows you so well and can still say that to you?

The "Small" Things Counts

Our God is good and righteous (Psalm 100:5; 143:10; Luke 18:19; 1 John 2:1). He can only do what is good and will never tempt you to do what is wrong (James 1:13-15). He is the source of victory, which meets a second basic human need – the need to feel significant, to know that we can do something positive with our lives. Because of Jesus, God has prepared "good works" for you to do (Ephesians 2:10)! These good works are not just the big things in life, like leading someone to faith in Jesus or giving a testimony before crowds of people. Good works, if they are done in His presence, can be as small as taking out the kitchen trash or sending someone an encouraging text message. As we listen to and follow Jesus, He can guide us in our good works throughout the day.

Your God also knows everything (Psalm 147:5; 1 Corinthians 2:11) and can give you the strength to accomplish the right thing (Job 42:2; Matthew 19:26). He is both omniscient and omnipotent. There is not a thought you've thought that He doesn't know about. There isn't a situation you face that's a surprise to Him. You can walk in peace knowing there are no unforeseen events with God, and that He can guide you through any situation. He knows everything, all the options, all the "what ifs," and even all the "woulda shoulda coulda's" as well.

He Alone Has the Power to Deliver

God may know everything, but what difference does that make when my life gets tough? In contrast to humans, God not only knows the right thing to do, but also has the power to make it happen. He alone can do the impossible, like giving life to a dead man (John 11:43-44). Our God knows all about tomorrow and eternity. He has the power to make even the bad situations you encounter work out for your good (Romans 8:28). You and I can't see around any corner, but He can, and the corner after that and the one after that as well. He sees everything, and will accomplish His purposes despite what humanity does (Proverbs 19:21). This relates to our third basic need – to feel safe and secure.

Galatians 5:22-23 states that when we walk in the presence of God, in the Spirit's power, we will experience love, joy, peace, patience, kindness, goodness, faithfulness, gentleness and self-control. Do you want to feel love, even when surrounded by people who have a hard time loving? Walk in the presence of your God, who cares so much for you. Do you want to feel peace, even on a stressful day? Walk in the presence of your God, who can give you the power to deal with that stress. Do you want to feel joy, even when circumstances are difficult? Walk in the presence of your God, where joy is found.

Jesus rubs off on us more and more as we walk in His presence. Psalm 9:3 tells how our enemies fall away at *His presence*, which brings us security. If you start to feel insecure, Psalm 16:11 reveals that there is joy *in His presence*. If you're feeling upset, there is protection *in His presence* (Psalm 31:20). If you're feeling discouraged, there is power to handle any situation *in His presence* (Psalm 97:5). If you're feeling inept, there is love and acceptance *in His presence* (Psalm 139:7).

Take the Next Step – Know Your God

For some people, it's hard to be in the presence of someone they don't know. For others, it's easy to be in the presence of unfamiliar people. Either way, trusting a stranger with your life would be a huge challenge. It simply is easier to be with someone you know and trust.

This is what your God is asking you to do – know and trust Him. And *the bigger your view of your God is, the smaller your challenges become.* Is your God big enough to trust?

Here's an easy way to find out. Ask yourself, "The last time I felt alone, insecure or insignificant, where did I turn – to Jesus, to myself, or to my drug of choice?" If to yourself, you need to know something new about your God. Spend time in His Word and ask Him to reveal the truth about Himself that you need to know. When He does, focus on this truth the next time you face a similar situation. As you do, you'll experience what you're looking for in life because your God was big enough to trust.

Chapter 3

When Your God Speaks, Are You Listening?

Faith is useless until you use it, until then it's just religion.

"The Spirit told Philip, 'Go to that chariot and stay near it.'" (Acts 8:29)

"Keep going forward." This is what I "heard" as I was surrounded by nothing but water. It had been raining hard in our area for a few days, which caused me to doubt whether I should even take this prayer walk. Rain can turn the grassy hills around my house into wonderful shades of green, but it can also turn the dirt trails into slippery, oozing mud. There is even one particular open space where deep craters become filled with water during the rainy seasons. As I was returning home from this particular prayer walk, I encountered the voice of God in the midst of no place to go, but back.

Right as I was about to turn around, I heard God say, "Keep going forward." I shook my head in surprise. *Really, God? All I can see is water*. If I followed what I heard, I would have to either walk on the water (which would be a miracle I'd like to experience!) or walk through the water to get home. I don't know about you, but walking with wet shoes is not something I enjoy, especially with three-quarters of a mile to go.

Worst Case Scenario

Though it seemed crazy, I thought I'd take a chance on obeying what I thought I heard God say. The worst case scenario was that I would waste time coming to a dead end where I'd turn around, or where I'd get to walk on water!

I walked a few steps forward through some brush. When I finally ran out of dry road and still only saw water I heard God say, "Turn right." *Okay God, let's go.* The moment I turned right, thinking I was about to plunge into two feet of water, I noticed a bridge that someone had made from wood that had floated down stream. It had been invisible from where I was standing a few moments before. You should have seen the smile on my face! It was so cool to know that I had heard Jesus and followed Him that day. He could see that bridge. I couldn't. He knew it was there all along. I didn't. His written Word told me to listen to His voice and follow. I did and I felt like I walked on air (even better than walking on water!) the entire way home. *My God, the God of the universe, not only wants to have a personal walk with me, He wants to speak to me too!*

Is God Still Talking Today?

I believe our God still speaks to His children today. I'm not necessarily talking about an audible voice, though it could happen. I'm talking about the voice inside your head telling you to trust – or, in my case, to go straight and then turn right.

I believe this is what Paul meant when he wrote about keeping in step with the Spirit (Galatians 5:25). Proverbs 3:5-6 doesn't say our journey to be like Jesus will be a straight road. No, our journey will have quite a few curves. Jesus, however, can see around the curves and corners, help us avoid crashes, and give us directions. At times the directions are clearer than at others, of course. You may face a decision that your biblical filter provides general guidelines for, but nothing specific to your situation.

What do you do then? Some people will say, "God gave you a brain and expects you to use it!" Yes, God gave us brains, but who says our thinking is biblically accurate or that our perception of the situation is correct? Our brains have been stained by a sinful nature and years of exposure to lies. He tells us in the above passage from Proverbs to trust Him, not our brains. It says to lean on Him, not follow our understanding of the situation. He expects us to use Jesus and His truths to filter each situation we face, not our own thinking.

If we are honest with ourselves, we'd have to acknowledge that it's our own thinking that often leads us astray in the first place!

We're in deep trouble if we're left to our own brain power. God is the one who can make our paths straight, even when there are bends in the road that we can't possibly see around. He can, though. It's in our best interest to have a personal walk in the presence of God through listening to Him if we want to avoid life's crashes.

The Shepherd and His Sheep

"My sheep *listen to my voice*; I know them, and they follow Me," (John 10:27). Shepherding is not an easy job. Jacob gives us a little insight into a shepherd's life in Genesis 31:40, saying, "The heat consumed me in the daytime and the cold at night, and sleep fled my eyes." Jacob also had to deal with responsibilities and losses while the sheep were under his care, beyond the physical hardships of just caring for them.

Jesus refers to a shepherding tactic in John 10. In order to get some sleep and still protect the sheep, a number of shepherds could band together and build a pen with a gate. They would put all of their sheep within that pen, close the gate, and then rotate the shepherd guarding the gate. It was his job to stay awake while the others got some valuable shut-eye. When it was time for the shepherds to gather their flocks, they would simply call to their sheep. The only sheep that would follow a particular shepherd were his own sheep! They knew his voice and would follow while the sheep belonging to other shepherds would move away from him. The shepherd would talk to his sheep and they would fall in line behind him *because they knew his voice*. Jesus calls Himself the Good Shepherd – One who will do whatever it takes to protect His sheep. He was willing to lay down His life for them!

Will You Listen?

As our Shepherd, He wants us to know, listen to, and follow His voice every day everywhere. When you come to a bend in the road that you don't know how to handle, you can learn to keep walking in His presence instead of leaning on your ability to think it through. To do this, though, you have to ask yourself, "Do I believe He can or will speak to me today?"

From Day 1 He's been speaking through creation (Psalm 19; Romans 1:20). He's also been communicating directly with humanity since their first day on the planet (Genesis 1:26-31).

Sometimes He speaks in an audible voice as He did with Abraham (Genesis 12:1-3) as well as to the crowd at Jesus' baptism (Matthew 3:16-17). Sometimes He speaks through dreams like He did with Joseph (Matthew 2:20-24) or in visions like He did with Isaiah (Isaiah 6:1) and John (Revelation 1:12-17). Sometimes He has uses situations to communicate vital information as He did with Jonathan (1 Samuel 14:6-14), or speaks through His people (Proverbs 15:22; cf. Ephesians 4:15; Acts 21:10-11).[1]

That Soft Inner Voice

I know my God speaks. Though I've never heard His audible voice outside my head, I've definitely heard Him through dreams, and through my brothers and sisters in Christ. The main way He has spoken to me, though, is through a quiet inner voice (Isaiah 30:21). Sometimes it's difficult to know that it's His voice and not mine. I've found that the answer to that puzzle lies in the question, "Where do words come from?" They can be spoken or written, but they come from the mind of the person who is communicating. When we say we have the Word of God – the Bible – the very words on the page are God speaking to us. The Bible is essentially His voice to us. Therefore, the more I read His Word, the more I'll know His voice.

I believe it's difficult, if not impossible, to have a personal walk in the presence of God without the written Word of God. We need an absolute authoritative source by which to know what we are "hearing" is from Jesus. This is why we need to use our biblical tools/truths to filter out all the other voices, including our own, in order to hear from Jesus, our Good Shepherd.

Here's an illustration. In a crowded room where people are loudly talking over each other, I can still hear my children's voices. Their giggles of laughter or screams of fear can be heard through all the noise going on around me. How is that possible? *I recognize their voices because I spend time with them.* It's the same with God's voice. The more I'm in His Word, the more I'm able to filter out all the other voices clamoring for my attention. Then His words become clear to me.

This is the mystical side of walking in the presence of God. Listening to God can't be put into a test-tube or some scientific formula. It's a life-long journey of getting to know Him through His Word. This will open your mind to recognize His voice so that you will know when it's your God speaking to you. This part is crucial to your walk; there can be dire consequences if you don't!

From the book that talks about eternity past (Genesis) to the book that talks about eternity future (Revelation) God is speaking. God is talking with His creation at the beginning of the book, the end of the book, and everywhere in between. It's my belief that Jesus had the first and last words when it comes to the written Word of God.[2]

God Speaks to Those Who Want to Listen

God *spoke* directly with His creation. Genesis 1:3 reveals that "God *said*, 'Let there be light.'" He *told* Adam to take care of the garden and not to eat from one particular tree while doing it (Genesis 2:15-16). He then *told* Adam and Eve what their roles in the new world would be (Genesis 1:27).

He had a *conversation* with Cain about doing the right thing (Genesis 4:6). He *spoke* with Noah about building a ship that would save humanity.

He appeared to Abraham in his hometown in modern day Iraq and *told* him to move to the land that He would eventually give to the nation of Israel. He asked Abraham to listen and follow Him, which was exactly what Abraham did.

He did the same with Abraham's son Isaac (Genesis 26:2) and grandson Jacob (Genesis 28:13), who (however imperfectly) both listened to and followed their God.

The Lord continued *speaking* to His people, the nation of Israel, "through the prophets at various times and in various ways," (Hebrews 1:2). Why through the prophets and not to the Israelites directly? It appears that most people were not personally walking in the presence of God and didn't want to hear from Him! From the time Joshua leaves the scene until the next "Joshua" comes (another name for Jesus) very few people are recorded as having *talked* with God directly (Israel in times of rebellion[3], certain judges[4], Samson's parents[5], certain kings[6]).

Communication with God continued after Pentecost when the Holy Spirit came to live inside believers. The Spirit told Philip in Acts 8:29 to go to the desert road and approach a chariot. Because he did, a royal Ethiopian official became a believer and shared about Jesus when he got home! Jesus ended up *talking* to Paul (Acts 9:4-6), because believers were afraid to go near him. Jesus also *told*

Paul his life's purpose (Acts 22:21). The Spirit took Peter out of his comfort zone and sent him to Caesarea to have a conversation with a certain Roman Centurion (Acts 10:19). God went on to encourage the leaders at Antioch to send a few people to start reaching the entire Gentile world with the gospel of Jesus Christ (Acts 13:2). God also led a man named Agabus to warn Paul about what would happen to him if and when Paul went to Jerusalem (Acts 21:10-11).

People in Scripture are recorded as having heard from God outside the written Scriptures in order to personally walk in His presence every day everywhere.[7] He made His children to have a relationship with Him (1 John 1:3), which demands two-way communication. If our God wants us to do even the mundane things of life, like eating and drinking, in His presence (1 Corinthians 10:31), wouldn't He want to talk to us while we do them? I believe so. He wants to communicate with us because He wants us to have an abundant life, which means living it His way throughout each day, wherever we go.

How to Hear From Your God

We get what we expect. *If we don't think God speaks or we don't want to hear Him, we probably won't.* We see this in the life of young Samuel in 1 Samuel 3:1-10. He had to repeatedly wake up Eli because he thought it was Eli calling him. It took a few times for even Eli to realize what was happening and then teach Samuel how to respond to God when He spoke.

If we want to hear from God, it's important for us to "unbusy" ourselves. If you stuff your schedule too tight or are too focused on your daily lists, you may not even think of asking Him for help with decisions. You'll be just like Martha, who was so distracted by all her tasks that she couldn't focus on what Jesus was saying (Luke 10:38-42). If you're too busy to say a short prayer like, "Lord, please guide me as I process this situation through Your Word," you're too busy. If you're so rushed that you can't say, "Lord, speak through me to this person during my next appointment," you need to "unbusy" yourself. Try following the example of Jesus, who discussed everything with His Father, no matter how hectic life became (John 8:28-29). He was the ultimate "unbusy" busy person! If He could slow down throughout His day to hear from His Father, we can too.

Stop! You Don't Have All the Facts

Another obstacle to hearing from the Lord is that we think we know what to do or what God wants done. This presumption can cost us dearly, as it did with Joshua and the Israelite leaders – *twice*. The first time, they had just come off a rousing victory over Jericho and were about to enter the next battle against Ai. They were so confident in their ability to handle the situation that they forgot to ask God what His battle plans were. They subsequently lost the battle, costing the lives of thirty-six Israelite soldiers (Joshua 7:1-5), because they assumed they knew what God wanted.

The second time, Joshua and the Israelites relied on their own judgment in a decision instead of asking God for His. One day, a group of people came to the Israelite camp, saying they had traveled from a distant country. They showed off their moldy bread and empty crusted wineskins (which by the way, the Israelite leaders actually touched). The logical conclusion? The travelers were from a distant land, which would mean it was okay for the Israelites to make a treaty with their guests. God had only told them to not make a treaty with anyone living within the Promised Land, not outside it. To their regret, they found that the visitors were actually Gibeonites, a very strong nation living *within* Canaan (Joshua 10:2). The Israelites "did not inquire of the LORD" and there were consequences because they didn't.

It seems Joshua was just like us…a slow learner who made the same mistake more than once. He and the leaders trusted sensory information – their eyes, ears and fingers – more than their God. It's when we trust ourselves (pride) rather than asking God to show us (humility) that we get into trouble. When we trust in our strengths (or talents, feelings or opinions), we're most vulnerable.

Where's Your Trust?

This leads to another potential roadblock in listening to Jesus – our trust levels. Do you feel like you have to be in control of your life? It's easy to think that there would be no accidents if we were in total control of ourselves, our environment and the people around us. *We have to learn to accept the fact that being in control is an illusion.* Instead, we can turn to someone who is bigger than us and our circumstances – our God. He can take everyone's choices, even the bad ones, and use them for our good (Romans 8:28). This means we need to be willing to trust Him enough to listen, and to trust that what He tells us will be in our best interests to follow. This also means we have to stop putting our trust in our emotions – even the positive ones.

In the Gospels, we read the challenging story of Lazarus. Jesus learned that one of His best friends in the world, Lazarus, had died. What would you do in that situation? You'd probably pick up the phone and call! Since this wasn't an option back then, you would have to either go yourself or send someone in your place. Jesus did neither. Instead, He waited two days before heading over to the house (John 11:1-6). This passage doesn't say why Jesus delayed, but earlier in John it reveals that Jesus had a life habit of listening to His Father before He said or did anything (5:19).

Both positive and negative emotions can hinder you from hearing God. What is your first response when you get angry – to react or to listen? In James 1:19, God cautions us to be slow to anger and quick to hear. Jesus loved Lazarus so much that He wept over the loss of His friend, but He still listened to and followed His Father first. God may want you to follow your feelings sometimes. Just make sure you filter them through Him first. (A useful tip to remember is to **HALT** before making decisions when you're feeling **H**ungry, **A**ngry, **L**onely or **T**ired.)

Don't Rush When He Says, "Hush!"

One final thought on listening to your God. Sometimes, you won't hear anything. So wait. *At times God will test how much we want to listen.* Our God isn't a God on demand. He'll speak when He's ready. Therefore, there are times when we have to, "Be still and know that He is God." (Psalm 46:10) God is asking us to trust Him and His timing. The bigger the question you have for Him, the longer the wait might be. Remember, Jesus doesn't need us to do anything for Him. He wants us to do everything with Him. It's often not as much about the situation as it is about the relationship you're developing with Him through it.

Jesus calls us friends (John 15:14). He doesn't force His way in. He doesn't threaten or intimidate. He wants you to follow Him because you want to. And sometimes He says, "Hush." Are you willing to be still and continue to get to know your God, or will you keep going your own way? Every time you obey when you hear, and then see the results, it will reinforce your desire to listen to and follow Him the next time. This builds that trust-relationship with

Him. When we choose to ignore God's voice, we make it harder to hear Him the next time. If this has happened to you ask, "Did I obey what He told me to do?" If not, He may be waiting until you do.

You Become Like Who You Listen To

You have the privilege of walking in the presence of the Most High God. You've been given the mind and nature of the Living Word of God, Jesus Christ. You have the Spirit of God inside you, who wants to have a living relationship with you. A relationship where two people get to know each other on a personal basis, forming a friendship based in trust, based on two-way communication. We speak and listen. He speaks and listens. This is a healthy relationship.

Your ability to hear God speak is directly proportional to how often you listen and obey. "The more you seek to hear your God's voice in detail, the more effective you will be in your own calling. Guidance is not a game, it is serious business where [you] learn what God wants [you] to do and how He wants [you] to do it."[8]

Have I always "heard" correctly? Nope. But I did the day He said, "Turn right!" Do I still need to get better at hearing His voice? Yes, just like I still need to learn how to listen to my wife better after 26+ years of marital bliss. I'm still on this journey learning to hear my God's voice, both in the written Word and from the One inside me. I'm constantly getting better at using my biblical tools to filter out the things already in my head and the things that want to get in it.

Your God wants to say to you like He did to me, "Keep going forward." He can see what's ahead, and wants to show you the firm ground. He wants you to take that walk in His presence. He wants to speak to you through His Word, and at times in other biblical ways, so keep your ears open.

No Amen-Ending Prayers

Think about this for a moment. Where in Scripture does it ever instruct us to say, "Amen" at the end of a conversation with God? We have no record that Jesus taught His disciples to say it (Matthew 6:9-14). Paul said in 1 Thessalonians 5:17, "Pray *continually*,...for this is God's will for you in Christ Jesus," (emphasis added). When does "continually" stop?

You have a personal God who wants to walk in close relationship with you. He cares about you and wants to be intimately involved in your daily life. He speaks to fill in the gaps where Scripture might only give general life principles. He speaks to guide you to the bridges you will need to walk over your challenges. It's time to put your faith to good use.

Take the Next Step – Listen to Your God!

Get used to His voice by reading Scripture daily. The Bible is God's Word, His voice speaking to you. While it may be easy to just flip it open now and then, or skip from one spot to another, you'll benefit much more if you read it in a scheduled way and not haphazardly. There are many good read-the-Bible-in-a-year programs out there.[9] Find one and get started listening to Jesus.

As you read, don't get too focused on understanding everything. There will be other times and places to study the Bible. Your personal time in and with the Word is not that time. It's about listening and recognizing His voice in your life. When you sense Him "speaking" or something "hits" you, stop and listen. You'll have times of conviction, encouragement, comfort, lies exposed, truths revealed, etc. – don't pass those by.

As you walk with Jesus throughout your day, have a running conversation with Him. He is your friend and is a good listener. There might be times when you'll hear, "Turn right." You're not crazy! The more you use your biblical tools to filter out all the other voices, the more His voice will become familiar to you.

"Keep going forward." *Really, God? All I can see is water.*
The pond created by all the rain.

Chapter 4

Life is About the Relationship, not the Destination

Don't wait until heaven to start looking into Jesus' eyes.

"No one gets to the Father except through Me." (John 14:6b)

"What a gorgeous view!" I said to my wife Jan as we walked along a beautiful stretch of the Inyo National Forest in California. We set off on this particular walk from our rustic, no-frills cabin with only a bottle of water each, my walking app, and each other. We had no particular destination in mind. We just wanted to take a walk with Jesus and each other. We'd let the scenery dictate the route.

A Walk with Jesus and Jan

This initially led us on a gravel road with slight uphill grade and tall Jeffrey pines, a few green Douglas firs turning into bright yellow leafed aspens on each side. The air was crisp and the conversation was great. About three-quarters of a mile on our way, we saw a dirt road leading to Sherwin Creek. We thought it would be nice to see if the creek had any fish swimming around in it, so we headed that direction.

After taking a few wrong turns that forced us to back track, we finally heard and eventually saw the snow-melt water. Then we decided to leave the trail to follow the creek. We laughed and talked as we plotted our way over the boulders and through the low-lying brush and fallen trees. At times we stopped to listen to the quickly moving water and look at the clear blue sky through the yellowing aspen leaves.

I had previously mountain biked in this area, so I knew there were fire roads not too far from our location. After enjoying this part of the creek, we decided to go find the fire road that had to be just north of us. Little did we know what lay ahead. The drought in this area, which had been going on for a few years, had been causing the trees to weaken and die. Foresters came through, cut down the trees, chopped them into three-foot sections, and then left them all over the place! Needless to say, the walking was less than ideal. With each new step, we had to look up to see where we were heading, as well as down to choose where to put our feet. We exchanged looks. *"What have we gotten ourselves into? Who had the bright idea to go this direction?"*

A Pleasant Path

Finally, after about 45 minutes, we reached the fire road, a pleasant area for our feet and eyes. As we continued walking, and talking about anything and everything, we started to hear the creek again. After about another half-mile we could see a line of yellow, green and brown aspen groves blowing in the breeze. *Let's head back to the water! We can refill our water bottles and cool off by putting our feet into the water.* We took the first trail heading toward the trees. Sure enough, once we hit the tree line we could see the fresh white water bouncing off the rocks in the stream. After soaking our feet in the mountain-fed creek, we put our shoes back on and headed back to the cabin. We weren't entirely sure of the way, though we knew the direction and, of course, we had the walking app.

After talking it over, we picked what looked like a trail through a meadow of low-lying brush. We soon realized that the trail really wasn't a trail at all. It was a deer path that wasn't always going the right way. After walking through the scratchy brush for a while, we were relieved to finally make it to the road.

Silence is Okay

Our conversation started to die down as fatigue set in. The sights were as gorgeous and the smells just as mountain-fresh as when we started two hours earlier, but we were tired from all the hiking and decision making. That last stretch toward home was a good ending, though. It was just the two of us with Jesus, and a quiet feeling of satisfaction.

Jan and I still remember this hike with fondness, even though there was nothing spectacular about it. It was never about the destination – it was about our relationship. We had our walking app so we never felt lost, and having it gave us the freedom to take paths we might not normally have taken. Without it, we might have missed the adventure of fallen trees and leg-scratching brush!

Building a Relationship

Our personal walks in the presence of our God are not about the destination. They are about the relationship that is built while taking the journey together now. A common belief is that Jesus came just to get us into heaven. But He makes a very interesting statement in John 17:3, saying, *"Now this is eternal life: that they may know You, the only true God, and Jesus Christ."* Jesus didn't say He came to save us from hell! No, He came to bring us into relationship with the Father and Himself.

Our time on this planet is not so much about where we're going when we die, but about Whom we're walking with! If we choose to walk with Jesus now on earth, we get to walk with Him for eternity. If we choose not to walk with Jesus now, we've also chosen not to walk with Him for eternity. This is a pretty good definition of hell on earth as well as after death; shut out from His presence and excluded from real life for eternity.

You're Already in His Presence

When we choose to experience the presence of God, it's only the beginning. We will get to continually experience it for eternity. It's one mountain-fed creek, one beautifully blue sky, one breezy aspen tree experience after another. Remember, the Bible is simply too small to tell us everything about our God. John writes, "Jesus did many other things as well. If every one of them were written down, I suppose that even the whole world would not have room for the books that would be written," (John 21:25). I imagine John is exaggerating to make a point, which is this: the written Word of God contains only a tiny fraction of information about who our God is and what He has, is and will do. The beauty is that we get eternity to experience more and more of Him!

I often have this conversation with believers.

"I can't wait to get to heaven," they say.

"Where is heaven?" I ask.

"Where God is."

"And where is God right now?"

I'm often met with a very puzzled look. Then it finally sinks in, while a smile spreads across their faces. *Our God is with us, living inside us as believers, right now.* Yes, one day we will leave this planet and go "home" where the separation between us and God will be gone. Let's not, however, forget that we can enjoy His presence *now.* Life is not about some far-off destination where God is, or about getting a reward when we die. It's about becoming more like Jesus as we walk in relationship with Him right now.

"They Hung out with Jesus!"

I love the distinguishing mark of the early disciples of Jesus. In Acts 4 we see John and Peter jailed for telling people the amazing story of Jesus and what He offered through His death and resurrection. The Jewish leaders questioned them at length. Acts 4:13 reads, "When they saw the courage of Peter and John and realized that they were unschooled, ordinary men, they were astonished and they took note that *these men had been with Jesus,*" (emphasis added).

They could see these men were not trained, but were regular everyday people. What got their attention was that Peter was talking to them as if he was a bona fide scholar, and even quoting the Hebrew Scriptures! The leaders realized something else about these two disciples – *they had been with Jesus.* To be more precise, Peter and John walked day-to-day with Jesus. Where He went, they went. Where He stayed, they stayed. When He taught, they listened. They were in step with Him. Because of this relationship, they were able to stand up to those who persecuted them for what they believed and taught about Jesus.

Religion or Relationship?

It's been said, rightly, that Christianity is not a religion, but a relationship. These believers were living examples of that. *Are we?* The Jewish leaders saw that Peter and John had been with Jesus. *Can those around us say the same thing about us?*

My wife and I don't remember all the things we talked about on our walks. We do remember, though, that we enjoyed ourselves. We look forward to more walks together, though the point is not the destination, or even the beautiful scenery – it's about doing something that brings us closer to each other. This is why Jan and I got married in the first place – to share life together.

Take the Next Step – Walk with Jesus Now

Jesus came to share life – His life – with us. Jesus wants to hang out with you today, not just once you arrive in heaven. Your eternal relationship with Jesus starts the moment you put your faith in Him as your Lord and Savior. *He wants to make that relationship stronger and more satisfying with each passing day.*

Are you walking the talk or just talking the walk? How would your friends respond if you asked them, "Do you see a Jesus in me that you would want to spend time with?" If yes, keep walking with Jesus! If not, you know what you need to work on! Why not start today?

Our no-frills cabin in the
Inyo National Forest in California.

Chapter 5

A Walk Focused on Jesus

Jesus doesn't add Himself or new behaviors to me. He replaces me with Him.

You become like what you focus on and what you focus on only gets bigger.

"Fix your eyes on Jesus, the author and perfecter of our faith." (Hebrews 12:2)

*I*t's so green everywhere! I was prayer walking in Murfreesboro, Tennessee, and the color of the grass reflected that this town was still in the midst of its rainy season. Back home the hills were already brown, so you can imagine how happy I was to see the lush green surroundings. I had been to Tennessee before, but I didn't get around much unless it was in a car. This time I was in the state to speak at a conference, but I have learned that if I want to stay closer to Jesus, prayer walking is too valuable a tool to neglect, even when traveling. Since I didn't know the area, I turned on my handy walking app and headed out, hoping it would let me track where I was and how to get back to where I was staying.

Walk in a New Neighborhood

This new neighborhood had a few surprises for me, besides the beautiful green. About half way through my walk, what appeared to be a German Shepherd started running toward me, baring its teeth and barking loudly. Thankfully, it lost interest soon, and I didn't have to fight it off, though my adrenaline was pumping.

As my heart returned to normal, I turned the corner to suddenly see something that, according to my app, didn't exist – a row of bushes and trees! I thought about turning around, but curiosity got the best of me. So I kept walking to see why there were trees in the middle of my road.

When I got closer, I discovered a dirt path on either side. Now my curiosity was really piqued. It wasn't until I followed the path that I realized the road did continue, but on the other side of the block of trees! I could only guess why this was done, but I was able to keep walking despite the difference between the app and reality.

Life's Guardrails

This prayer walk highlights an important insight into walking in the presence of our God. *A rule-based life will never get us where we want to go; we need God to speak.* Just like my app didn't show the trees in the middle of the road, the Bible doesn't have a chapter and verse for every single one of life's potential detours. Not every situation you will face on your walk with Jesus is specifically covered in the Bible. This is why God created humanity to live in His presence and follow Him. We wouldn't really need to walk in His presence if we had detailed instructions on how to handle life's daily challenges. A walk based on relationship is living and breathing, where a rule-based one can become mechanical and dead.

Don't misunderstand; we need the Word of God! It is *the* primary source for hearing the voice of God. Like a friend of mine once said, "It talks!" It is *the* only source of truth that enables us to filter out all the other voices vying for our attention. It is the source of truth that enables us to withstand our enemy's attacks. It is the sole authority for living in the presence of God.

The written Word of God, however, is like the guardrails on a mountain road. Just as we're glad those rails are there to protect us from falling off a cliff, we can be grateful God gave us scriptural boundaries to protect us from destroying our lives. The Bible does get very specific on which behaviors to avoid, since by doing them we hurt ourselves, and our relationship with others and Jesus. *There is freedom in choice, but not in consequences.* We need those guardrails, but we don't focus on them while we're driving. We keep our eyes on the road and enjoy the sights along the way. Jesus is that road. He is the scenery. He is *the Way* and *the Truth* and *the Life* (John 14:6). He is the Word of God (John 1:1,14) and wants His sheep to listen to Him throughout their day. He wants us to focus on Him rather than on a set of do's and don'ts. The written Word of God is very specific on how we as believers are to filter out the various messages vying for our attention so we can walk in the presence of

God. The key, however, is where we focus – on the rules or on the relationship.

Jesus' Focused Life

Jesus modeled this way of walking with God for us. In John 5:19 He said, "I tell you the truth, the Son can do nothing by Himself; He can do only what He *sees* His Father doing." Later, in John 8:28, He said, "I do nothing on My own but speak just what the Father has *taught* Me." He takes this a step further in John 12:49, saying, "I did not speak on My own accord, but the Father who sent Me commanded Me *what to say and how to say it*," (emphasis added).

Notice what He didn't say. He didn't say, "I only do what the Scriptures tell Me to do." Instead He said, "I do what I see and hear My Father doing." This is exactly what He told His disciples to do.

Did He know the Scriptures? He certainly did. He knew where to find appropriate passages (Luke 4:17-21) and the meaning behind all that was written (Matthew 5:21-22; 27-28). He had specific Scriptures in His shield of faith in order to defeat His enemy (Matthew 4:1-11)! It's what He did first that's of importance here, though – listening and following. He lived in complete relationship with His Father, focusing on Him and not on the rules themselves. This is why I believe Jesus said what He did. He wasn't downgrading Scripture. He was elevating the relationship aspect of what the Scriptures taught in order to bring back what had been misplaced over time. Throughout Scripture – the Old and New Testaments – God's desire for us has been to live in relationship with Him, both for ourselves and in community.[1]

There's No Rule Book Big Enough

Because we were meant to live in Jesus' presence and because He wants to speak with us, He wants us to stay focused on Him, not the rules. So when did "religion" begin? When did rules become the focus rather than being in relationship with Him? You might have guessed the answer: the Garden of Eden.

God set up the guardrails in Genesis 1-2. Adam and Eve were given only four rules to guard their walk. They were to have children, rule the planet, subdue those out of line and not eat from one certain tree in the garden. Sounds simple, right? It was, and should have been until the catastrophic events of Genesis 3 took place. Adam and Eve were faced with a challenging situation – a devious talking serpent. Scripture doesn't say this was the only animal that ever talked. It doesn't say if this was the first time Satan (Revelation 12:9) had ever talked to them. What it does say is that this animal had ulterior motives. He was cunning and on the attack (Genesis 3:1).

We don't read of any specific instructions from God on how to handle this situation, no rulebook to fall back on when it came to talking snakes. So what should Adam and Eve have done? They should have talked to God, rather than just with each other. They were created to be in relationship with God. All they had to do was ask, "Hey, Father, what's up with the talking snake? What should we do?" If they had, we might not be where we are today. What they did instead was disastrous for them and for all of us. They ignored God and thought they could handle the situation on their own. They ate from the forbidden tree. Then they tried to deal with the consequences by covering up their mistake (in this case with clothes made of sewn fig leaves). Voilà! A rules-based, human-centered religion was born. Humans decided they could choose whom to listen to and whom to follow in handling everyday situations.

Focus on Relationship Rather Than Rules

As far as Scripture tells us, God had not given any more instructions on how to live by the time the next walk-with-God character, Enoch, arrived on the scene. The Mosaic Law with the Ten Commandments didn't come until centuries later, so how did Enoch live?

Relationship. This relationship was so tight that God took Enoch to heaven without Enoch ever experiencing physical death. What did Enoch focus on? Relationship. How did Enoch handle daily life? Relationship.

As believers, we're supposed to walk the same way. Hebrews 3:1 reveals that believers are to "fix your thoughts on Jesus, the apostle and high priest whom we confess." As *the* apostle, He can show us how to live. As *the* high priest, He can reconcile us when we turn our backs on God. The writer goes on to say, in Hebrews 12:2, "Fix your eyes on Jesus, the author and perfecter of our faith." To fix your eyes, you have to be facing toward God. This face-to-face encounter is all about relationship, which is exactly the opposite of what got humanity in trouble. Adam and Eve turned their backs on God and focused on someone and something else.

If we want to enjoy the good things God has for us, we need to focus on listening to and following Jesus. He gave us our faith and is fully capable of making it complete. Jesus didn't come to add another layer of behaviors/rules for those who follow Him. He came to replace our worn out, temporary character with His own. He wants to remove the faulty thinking that leads to faulty behaviors.

A rule-based life is like eating junk food. The calories give you an immediate high, and burst of feel-good energy, but it leaves you empty afterward. Jesus said, "I am the Bread of Life. Listen to and follow Me and you will be satisfied both now and forever" (John 6:35 paraphrased).

Our Character or His?

Jesus wants us to walk in newness of life, to replace our character with His (not just add new behaviors to us) so we can walk closer to Him. He wants us to spend time reading the Bible so we'll begin to think like Him and can better hear His voice. He wants to remove anything and everything that gets in the way of our relationship with Him. He wants to change us from the inside out by changing the way we think and choose (Romans 12:2). We can become like Him and take Christ-like character with us into eternity!

Sometimes it is easier to live by rules. A rule-based walk keeps us in control. *Good Christians go to church services. I went to service this past week. Therefore, I am good and God should be happy with me.* Ironically, it's possible to go to a service but turn your back on Him by ignoring Him the whole time. He wants us to "fix our eyes" on Him, not the show, so we can hear from and follow Him every day everywhere. This is much harder to do and much harder to regulate than following rules. It's important to remember that rules are there to keep us from doing things that would hurt us and others, not necessarily to help us become like Him.

Even Our "Oops" Are Covered

I find it interesting that God, in Leviticus 4, had a specific sacrifice for what I call the "oops" sins. It was called the sin offering for unintentionally committed sins. It was for the "Sorry, I didn't know that was wrong" or "should have done, but didn't do" sins. Even when they didn't know they had walked away from God's presence, this sacrifice allowed the Israelites to come back into it. Jesus' sacrificial death does the same for the believer today. We hurt God all the time without even knowing it. He knows we can't live a life based on do's and don'ts – we were never meant to know what all the do's and don'ts were in the first place! We are still responsible for these "unknown" mistakes, but Jesus' sacrifice covered them, so we too can stay in the presence of God.

Jesus Is Looking for Belief

Once Jesus was asked by a large group of people, "What must we do to do the works God requires?" His answer probably shocked the crowd. He answered simply, "The work of God is this: to *believe* in the one He has sent," (John 6:25-29, emphasis added). They wanted to know what they had to *do* to walk with God. They wanted to know what rules they had to follow and what good deeds they had to perform for God to be pleased with them. Jesus was putting their eyes back on the One who counts – Himself.

Believing in Jesus is not just for salvation; it's also for sanctification – becoming more like Him. Paul took up this argument in his letter to the Galatians. He called them fools for forgetting what he had taught them (Galatians 4:1). He spent a great deal of ink and parchment to emphasize a very important truth: *we started our walk with God by faith and we need to keep walking the same way.* By faith, we are seated with Him in the very throne room of God, the real Holy of Holies (Ephesians 2:6). Why then would you feel like you had to "do something" for Jesus to stay there? Paul asked the Galatians (and generations of believers afterward), "Why would you want to go back to slavery?"

Take the Next Step – Stay Focused on Jesus

Jesus came so we could have a relationship with the Father through faith. He started the job and He will finish the job – by Himself (Philippians 1:6). Our job is to stay focused on Him and follow His leading. We were saved to focus on Jesus, not the rules. We were created to look into His eyes and let His voice become clearer.

My friends, we become like what we focus on and what we

focus on only gets bigger. Where's your focus today – your rules for "successful Christian living" or Jesus? Are you clearing your decisions through Him or a rulebook? Get Jesus in focus by picking up your biblical tools to screen out everything else so you can listen to and walk with Him wherever He goes.

Chapter 6

Drawing Closer

Jesus came to give you an abundant life, not the good life.

"Come near to God and He will come near to you." (James 4:8)

What a sight it was, as dusk fell and the night air turned cold. Picture about twenty guys in the middle of nowhere, surrounded by tall pines, manzanita bushes, and lots of rocks and dirt. Our men's retreat one spring was held in a primitive camping location in the mountains. Primitive camping meant the campsite had zero amenities – no toilets, showers, or electricity. The only perk that came with the site was a fire ring.

A Rip-Roaring Fire

We men tend to do things much bigger than ever needed, including building a fire. In all honesty, we did need one to keep us warm once the night air started sending chills through our bones. When the fire detail started the fire, they couldn't leave well enough alone; if a little was good, a lot was better. We had a rip roaring-fire before we knew it! A few brave souls tried to get close to the red-hot flames, but soon even they had to move away after the rubber soles of their shoes started to melt and their pants started getting attacked by flying sparks!

What was interesting to watch, however, was the movement of the men and their camping chairs. After the fire became a bonfire, everyone found a comfortable distance from the roaring flames. As their bodies adjusted to the fire's heat, and the cold air began to seep through their sweatshirts, they started to pick up their chairs and edge closer to the flames. Then after adjusting to the new comfort level, their skin would eventually start to exhibit goose bumps, and they would pick up their chairs and walk still closer to the fire ring.

Get Warm or Stay Cold

The guys had a decision to make each time they began to shiver. They could stay at a distance from the fire, get colder, and put on more clothes. Or, they could pick up their chairs and walk closer to the fire.

These are the same options those who want a personal walk in the presence of their God have. Jesus is that warming fire. Jesus makes us "wholly" through faith in Him at the moment of salvation. Because of this "wholliness," we can come into the very presence of God, the fire that keeps us warm on a cold night. He is the only One who can give us the warmth of security and significance in the midst of a cold insecure world.

Wholly? Wholliness? I chose those words on purpose. The biblical term "holy" means more than just not sinning. It also carries the idea of being made clean, purified or made whole again by separating out the bad stuff. We see this in the process of gold refining. Often fire is used to remove the impurities contained within the gold. The gold is now whole; it is holy, or separated from impurities, and made clean. It's wholly pure.

Dirty or Clean Water

Say you have a water bottle filled with purified water and are casually walking down the street drinking it. Then you notice two things. One, you're running low on water; and two, there is water in the gutter that runs along the sidewalk. Instead of having to go home to refill, you could choose to put that gutter water into your bottle. The problem is, you may have more water than you had before, but even what you had before has become undrinkable. You can't make more clean water by adding dirty water to it. Instead, you make the clean water dirty.

Let's reverse this process. Say you add your clean water to the dirty gutter water. What do you get? The same result – more dirty water! The only way to make that gutter water clean and drinkable is to purify it. God is not only clean, but He is also holy, meaning completely separated from any imperfection. God is so holy that

He will never contaminate Himself by allowing impurity into His presence.

We also see this idea of purity in the biblical concepts of clean and unclean. Under Old Testament law, an unclean person was shut out of the presence of God. In order to be restored, they had to stop the action that made them dirty, and in some cases wash themselves. Then they had to offer a sin (or *purification)* sacrifice and a burnt (or *come near)* sacrifice.[1] One sacrifice made them pure, and another made them holy, which gave them the ability to come back into the presence of God again. Jesus, however, became the ultimate sacrifice and offered believers both results – purification and reconciliation. God made us "*holy* through the sacrifice of the body of Jesus Christ once for all...because *by one sacrifice* He has made perfect forever those who are being made holy," (Hebrews 10:10b,14, emphasis added).

Continual Process of Being Made Pure

For anyone to see God, let alone walk with Him, they have to be both pure *and* whole/holy. God permanently handled both for us by sending Jesus, whose life and death washed us and made us holy. On the one hand, we are holy right now; and on the other hand, we are still in the process of being made holy. This may sound like a contradiction, but it's not. And the key lies in the bonfire illustration.

The believer is made whole the moment they put their faith in the sacrificial death of Jesus on the cross. Because of this, the believer can now come into the very presence of God and enjoy the flame of that rip-roaring fire...at a distance!

As long as we live on this planet we will be in the *process of being made holy*. We are *already considered* holy so we can enjoy the warmth of His flame. This is what brings security and significance. We are simultaneously *being made* holy so we can constantly come closer to the flame without melting our shoes and burning holes in our clothing. Holiness is both a one-time act and a process. This makes it possible to stay near the flame, and at the same time, it's a process in which we are continually getting closer to the source of that flame – Jesus.

The Decision to Draw Near to Jesus

Believers have a choice each time they face situations that make them uncomfortably cold. They can ignore Jesus and stay cold. (I call these Christian agnostics. They believe in Jesus, but ignore Him or believe He doesn't want to help them.) Believers can try to handle situations themselves, which only delays the chill. Or, they can do what James says in the Bible, "Come near to God and He will come near to you. *Wash* your hands you sinners, and *purify* your hearts, you double minded," (James 4:8, emphasis added).

Notice the wording James uses. *You can wash* (be made clean) and *purify* (be made whole) yourself by separating yourself from what made you dirty in the first place. Every day, everywhere, we have choices to make. We can choose to walk closer to God's flame, and experience the good things that come from walking in His presence. Or, we can choose to stay at a distance and be temporarily warm (since sin is fun for a little while) before getting very uncomfortable with the way our lives are turning out. Since God wants us to walk in His presence, He'll use various methods to get us to *want* to come closer to Him, or to draw us back when our walk starts to meander away from Him.

Realize You're Cold!

On our retreat, the guys didn't know to pick up their chairs and walk closer to the fire until they started feeling cold. They only knew that once they were warm, but now they were cold. There is just something about us humans that resists moving until we have to. It's not always that we don't like change; it's just that we don't like *being* changed. We all like our routines. We like being comfortable right where we are, but our God wants to draw us closer to Him. So, in His great love for us, He uses the coldness of life, the hard times, to get our attention. Without those, we would likely stay in our chairs at the same distance from the fire. We would miss all the good things that come from being closer to Him.

We only know what we know when we know it. What gets us to realize that there's more to personally walking in the presence of God than we're currently experiencing? Challenges. Jesus didn't come to give us an easy life. He came to bring us an abundant life! Love is found in the presence of God, not in more stuff. Joy is found in the presence of God, not in perfect health. Peace is found in the presence of God, not in more money. Security and significance are *only* found in the presence of God.

Drawing Closer

So what does God use to grow our thinking, to get us to move closer to Him? Life. The author of Hebrews 12:7 writes, "Endure hardship as discipline." God does this so "that we may share in His holiness." God wants us to be holy for the sole reason that it allows us to go deeper into our relationship with Him. He is removing the impurities so we can enjoy the "harvest of righteousness and peace for those who have been trained by it," (Hebrews 12:10-11).

How does it feel when you do the right thing? How does it feel to get closer to God? If we choose to take a step closer to the fire, the hardships and challenges will have been worth it. We are further refined so we can experience more of God. Jesus didn't come to *add* Himself or new behaviors to me. No, He came to *replace* me with Him. The abundant life means experiencing more joy, more peace, and more of God's presence. For most of us, though, it takes challenges or the cold night air to get us to move closer to God's warming flame.

The "good life" of this world is temporary. Health will not last, as everyone dies. Any wealth will only be left for those who didn't earn it, if you can keep it that long. No, "the world and its desires pass away, but the man who does the will of God lives forever." (1 John 2:17) Living by any worldview other than a biblical one will not bring us what we're looking for in life. Sometimes it takes Jesus letting us get "cold" before we open our eyes. Then we can allow the Spirit of God to expose the lies in our heads and exchange them for the truth. The question, "Is it working for you?" is crucial. You live the way you do because that is where your thinking takes you. When you realize you're cold and that your way of living isn't working, you're ready for Jesus to draw you closer to the warming presence of God.

The Spirit Uses Others to Draw You Closer

Sometimes the Spirit will make a change in your thinking instantaneously, but usually He will use the process He set out in Scripture. He did this with the Israelites when they entered the Promised Land and He does it with the believer today.[2] God wants us to reclaim what Adam lost – the ability to choose to defeat our challenges by walking in God's presence.

It's not just about you and your life. Don't hide your journey to be like Jesus from others. For one thing, it is nearly impossible to become more like Jesus without others. For another, there are a lot of freezing people who don't know where the source of warmth is. They need to see with their own two eyes that *walking with Jesus is not a cheap cliché*. Walk with others so they can learn from you and you from them. Let others see your struggles so they can be comforted that they're not alone. Be an authentic Jesus believer.

Take the Next Step – Use Challenges to Draw Closer to Jesus

You don't actually arrive at the flame until you see Jesus face-to-face. Until then, it's your choice how you will deal with life's inevitable challenges. You can allow the Spirit to use them to purify you so you can draw closer to the warmth of Jesus. Or, you can fight what the Spirit is doing, stay where you are, and remain cold. You can choose to pick up your biblical tools and walk closer to Jesus, or leave them in your tool belt and keep your distance. It's your choice: warmth or cold. Make the wise choice – use your challenges to draw closer to Jesus! Others are watching, and just might pick up their chairs and join you!

Chapter 7

Living with Jesus Everywhere

Stop going to church…be the church everywhere.

We don't just spend time with God. We live with Him.

"Therefore go and make disciples…I am with you always, to the very end of the age." (Matthew 28:19a,20b)

Almost every day as I woke up in Israel I thought, "Man, I don't feel like walking today." I go on my prayer walks faithfully when I'm at home, but when I'm on the road it's a completely different story. And that's oh so true when I'm traveling in Israel.

Each year I help lead a trip through *Hope for Israel*. The participants who join us on this trip experience Israel's past, present and future. They encounter the culture and all the sights, sounds, smells, and savory tastes that go with it. It's a one-of-a-kind experience; people literally see the Bible go from black and white to 3D and HD color, as they travel through the cities and countryside that they had only ever read about.

One person who came with us said, "It's both exhaustive and exhausting!" We leave the hotel between 7-8 AM each morning and arrive back at the hotel in the evening to freshen up for dinner, which is at 7 PM. In between those times, the group is on the road, experiencing as much as they can mentally, physically, emotionally and spiritually absorb. It's so tiring that many of the travelers choose to sleep between stops!

Tired Excuses

As one of the trip leaders, I get up earlier and go to bed later than the group. Beyond that, there are leadership meetings, logistics, and jet lag. I'm in motion from the moment I meet the group in the States until the time I bring them back. It's tempting to ask myself, "Do I have the time or energy to squeeze in a prayer walk?" The better question, though, is, "How much of my God's presence do I want to experience?"

"I'm tired" is a plausible excuse, but an excuse nevertheless. I've heard excuses come in so many shapes and sizes but they boil down to this: "I don't have time to spend with God!" This excuse has a fatal flaw. *It assumes that God wants my time in the first place.* Yes, you read that correctly. God doesn't want my time. He wants me.

In Motion With Jesus

Adam and Eve were not created to sit on a mountaintop and contemplate their belly buttons. No, they had a job to do each day. A job that, if done in His presence, would bring a sense of fulfillment. Jesus didn't do what He did so believers could live relaxed, isolated lives here on earth. He came to put us into relationship with a very personal God who wants us to walk with Him every moment of the day. I repeat often – to anyone who will listen – that we are supposed to stop *going* to church and to start *being* the church instead.

I had finished speaking at a men's conference when a pastor came to me, shaking his head. "Stop going to church, huh?" he said as he walked by; I'm not sure whether he got the point I was trying to make. Here is the background. The English word "church" is not scriptural. It is merely the English translation of the Greek word *ekklesia.* The word "church" didn't even come into the *English* language until the Middle Ages, some time before the 12th century.[1] From then on it has taken on a life of its own.

Jesus Is Calling Us Out

For example, if your friends asked you, "Where do you go to church?" You'd likely give them the name of a building on a certain street in your town, and describe the service. This is not biblical thinking![2] This is Western Christianity thinking, which has greatly influenced the rest of the world. The English word "church" comes from the combination of two Greek works *ek* and *kaleo* to make *ekklesia. Ek* means to move away from a starting point, to move away from point A to another location B. *Kaleo* means to call out very loudly. Thus, an *ekklesia* is a group of people who are called out from one location to another.

Jesus uses this word in Matthew 16:18, referring to His group of called out ones. He is the One calling a certain group of people from one place. He is the One calling those who have put their faith in Him to come to Him, to be more like Him.

Furthermore, it's Jesus' church, not mine, yours or any pastor's. Jesus calls His sheep to move away from where they are to be where He is. He says, "Come to Me, all you who are weary and burdened, and I will give you rest. Take My yoke upon you and learn from Me, for I am gentle in heart, and you will find rest for your souls. For my yoke is easy and My burden is light," (Matthew 11:28-30).

Jesus Is Calling Every Day

Jesus is calling us to listen to and follow Him every day everywhere, not just when we gather at one specific location on one specific day. We are to be the church, a group of people who are continually going toward Him. Yes, we gather as a group of called out ones, whether it be in an olive grove, a car, an abandoned bomb shelter or a bright new building on 4th and Main Street. I strongly believe that believers need to gather, *but that service or gathering is not church*. It's a gathering *of* the church. We must learn to stop just *going* to church, which can lead to a Sunday-only faith. We are to *be* the church, which leads to an every day faith.

A Call to Live with Jesus

Jesus wants His followers to have a personal walk with Him, 24/7, until they eventually come into His presence in a place called heaven. Specifically, He calls us to walk with Him while being used by the Spirit to make more followers or "disciples" of Jesus. Adam and Eve were given a job to do while they walked in the presence of God, and so are we. Jesus said, "Go make disciples of all the nations." Everything we do should be about making disciples. In *Discipleship: Copies of the Original*, biblical discipleship is defined as "giving people the biblical tools so they can listen to and be in relationship with Jesus for themselves in community, and then follow Him throughout their day, not just when they gather for public worship."[3]

When we live with Jesus, our lives will be changed as our

characters are replaced with His. When this happens, those around us will see Jesus in us. As they see Him, and as we talk about what Jesus has done for us, He may use us to call them out to follow Him too. Evangelism is the very beginning of the biblical discipleship process. If and when they choose to follow Jesus, He can use us to pass along our biblical tools to them so they can personally walk in the presence of God. This is the continuing process of biblical discipleship: learning how to listen to and follow the One who calls us out.

Continually Learning About Jesus

Think about this. We learned in the last chapter that Jesus made us "wholly." We also learned that we are still in the process of being made holy today and will be made completely holy when we see Him. Since both are true, why are we left behind on this planet once we come to faith? While I'm sure there are many reasons, I want to share two: knowing our God and making disciples. We just talked about the second reason. There are plenty of people we know and spend time with who do not know or walk with Jesus personally. Some of them are waiting to see if Jesus really does work in the world in which they live. So, where would they see this if all the living examples were gone? The old cliché, *you may be the only Bible some will ever read,* is true. While we're living with Jesus in the middle of the "good works" He has for us to do, others can see Jesus in us and then learn how to follow Him for themselves. Jesus is inviting them to be in relationship with Him just as He invited us. He can use our changed lives and walks to do it.

This living example starts, though, with an often overlooked reason for God leaving us on this planet after coming to salvation – knowing Him. Our God has so much to teach us about Himself! Our journey to know our eternal God starts by living with and learning more about Him with each breath we take, no matter where that breath is taken – here or there. What I learn about and incorporate into my life today means I get to learn and incorporate something new tomorrow, and so on throughout eternity.

In a way, this is what 1 Corinthians 3:10-15 teaches us. As children of God, we are not judged as to our destiny, since we live on the secure foundation of Jesus Christ that comes through faith in Him (John 1:12). Children of God are, however, judged as to how they lived the lives God gave them. Some will have learned more about Jesus than others, and will start on the next leg of their journey at different spots. Some will be learning their ABC's of Jesus while others are learning their GHI's while others are on their RST's.

The Bible only gives us a small glimpse of who our God is. To think that it contains everything there is to know about God would be to insult Him. How much is there to learn about God the Father, God the Spirit, let alone about God the Son? We get the awesome privilege of being called out to listen to and follow Jesus. We're in the process of becoming more like Him, plus we get to experience the good things He has for us along the way.

This learning about Him can start right now. Your God doesn't want your time. He wants you. *Your God wants you to live with Him, not do things for Him.* He wants you to know Him now, not work to get something from Him later. We are secure children of God, not His workhorses. He has taken off the pressure to perform, which allows us to focus on Jesus, rather than our daily tasks, and to become like Him. *We need to learn to stop trying to be someone we're not and/or doing something to get something we already have – fulfillment in Christ* (Colossians 2:9). As this happens, we can be ready to share how He's changed our lives with those around us. Though, we can't convince them to believe in Jesus, we certainly can share what living in His presence has done for us. The more we wrap our heads around this truth, the more we'll enjoy living in His presence on this planet.

Take the Next Step – Evaluate Your Daily Schedule

Take a look at your schedule. Do you schedule God into your day when it's convenient for you or do you talk about your schedule with Him throughout your day? Is He one of your priorities or the keeper of your priorities when it comes to time usage? One approach is spending time with God; the other is living with Him in each moment of the day. You have to work toward the latter if you want to enjoy the good things Jesus came to give His sheep.

Man, I don't feel like walking today!
My wife and I on the next to last day of our trip.
Yes, those are smiles on our faces.
I couldn't have been too tired to get out and walk!

Chapter 8

A Walk of Continual Progress

Accept one another where you're at, though not liking what each other does, while lovingly nudging each other toward Jesus.

"Bear with each other and forgive whatever grievances you may have against one another. Forgive as the Lord forgave you. And over all these virtues put on love, which binds them all together in perfect unity." (Colossians 3:13-14)

*A*re we there yet? This phrase took an entirely different meaning on this particular prayer walk. We have some good-sized hills around our house; the elevation gains are anywhere from a few hundred to over a thousand feet. I have a few hiker friends who use them for training purposes. That was not the intent of this prayer walk, though. The three of us, my wife, my daughter, and I, wanted to walk from our house to the top of this one hill where a cross stood. Then we would walk back home. It was only 4.25 miles, round trip, but the elevation would be a challenge. Another challenge would be keeping focus, since the cross was only visible when starting the climb, and not during. Parts of the trail were clearly marked while other sections were much more difficult to see, let alone walk.

The Cross is Up There

So there we were, enjoying our walk in the presence of God when we came to "the hill." The first leg of the journey wasn't too bad. It was more of a fire road than a trail; you could tell someone tried to get up this hill in a truck. We were a little winded and our legs started to feel the strain of carrying our bodies up the incline. It only got steeper and harder from that point. *Do we really want to continue?* The three of us looked at each other and nodded. We were committed to getting to the top so we could sit by the cross and take in the awesome 360-degree view of the valley. We still couldn't see the cross. We only knew it was up there somewhere.

The next section was loose soil and gravel, which was a little harder, but on we went, only to come to a section that made a Stairmaster look easy! After making it through that part we took a little break to catch our breath and let our heart rates slow. We looked up. *Where is that cross? Where is the top?*

The next part of the climb was a long stretch. *We can gut out this section. We're almost there.* So we pushed on. The conversation was a little slower. The gasps for air were a little deeper. After about 15 minutes, we got to the top…of the rise! We still couldn't see the summit, but the next stretch in this trail looked like it might lead to it.

Stopping Isn't Worth It

This next section of our prayer walk was steep and covered in rocky, loose soil. *We're already getting tired. Why did we even take this trail?* We had to be on a constant lookout for solid footing; we didn't want to hit a patch of loose gravel only to find ourselves sliding and falling backwards. We definitely didn't want to have to retrace our steps after a fall.

As we took what we thought would be our last steps up the hill, we encountered another steep section, though it was a little firmer underfoot. We looked down. We looked up. *Why couldn't we have seen all this heartache before we started the climb?* Yet, we had to admit that the view was getting better with each ridge we conquered. We were also still enjoying talking with each other and with God as we went.

It actually felt harder on our legs to stop and start than to just keep going. *We're not going to stop anymore until we reached the top,* we decided. As we climbed, we became acutely aware that it was leading us to *the* top, though there was still one smaller hill to climb. With each step, the cross got bigger.

The Joy of the Climb

After conquering the last hill it was only a matter of a few more steps on rubbery legs to the cross. We made it! A good wind was blowing our hair. We saw a green golf course that ran through a housing tract, the sun shining off lake water, brown farm land all around and even more hills! Our shirts were wet with sweat. Our water bottles were running low. Our legs let us know they had been abused. Our hearts were still returning to a regular rhythm, but we had done it. My daughter even took a picture of my wife and me to prove it! We climbed the hill and stood by the cross with a sense of accomplishment. We felt like we were at the top of the world even though it was only a few hundred feet above where we started.

Along the way, we could have focused on all the "hardships" and aches and pains, or we could have focused on the top where the cross was. We could have focused on the disappointments along the way, or we could have kept going. This is a fair description of a personal walk in the presence of your God. Will we focus on our imperfections or on Jesus? Will we concentrate on our aches and pains, or on the joys that come from living with Him?

Stronger for the Walk

Walking up that hill was enjoyable and excruciating at the same time. We conquered that hill, and were physically and mentally stronger for it. The same is true for everyday life. The Bible commands us in Philippians 4:4-5 to stop focusing on our challenges and complaints. Instead we are to rejoice in the Lord because He is near! We have the awesome privilege of walking in the presence of our God.

Contrary to the belief of many, this planet is under the control of our adversary, Satan, (Ephesians 2:2). He is not a cruise director, working to make our lives enjoyable! He knows he can't keep believers from getting to heaven, but he can make our lives a living hell, *if* we let him. In answer, Paul tells us to "rejoice in the Lord always." He repeated himself to make sure we got the point, "I will say it again: Rejoice!"

We are on a journey of becoming more like Jesus (1 John 3:1-3). We are to always have His praises on our lips (Psalm 34:1). We are to continually pray and give thanks (1 Thessalonians 5:17). We live each day with both good and bad, most of which is beyond our control. We do, however, have total control over our attitude. Using the **FREE**dom process, we choose where our minds will rest. Will we focus on the cross at the top of the hill, or on our aching legs and thumping hearts? Will we focus on the source of our salvation and hope, or on our challenges and complaints? Your brain will go where *you* tell it to – up or down.

Life is a Work in Progress

We didn't get to the top of the hill in one jump. It was one steady step after another all the way to the top. We walked up the hill together with Jesus. We could have focused on the slippery gravel and slips and falls. Instead, we enjoyed His presence in the midst of them on the way up.

I love how the Spirit describes this part of our personal walk in the presence of our God in Colossians 3:1-4. "Since, then, you have been raised with Christ, set your hearts on the things above, where Christ is seated at the right hand of God. Set your minds on things above, not on earthly things." The word "raised" is in the past tense – it's already completed. The top is not just a goal – it's a reality. We're still climbing, but we're also already there! That's how our focus can be on "the things above." Why get upset over the aches and pains of living on this planet when we are already victorious over them? In Christ, we win.

You Will Make it to the Top

The Spirit also tells us why we should keep our focus there. It's where Jesus is – at the right hand of God. The right hand means power and authority. Not only do I have God the Son, helping me up the hill of life, but God the Father as well! Daily living in the presence of your God can be tough. Still, we're walking with Someone who keeps telling us, "Don't stop. It hurts more if you do. Keep going. I'm with you, but I'm waiting for you at the top as well. I'll help you make it up by giving you the strength to take one step after another. You will make it!"

This fact is stated in Colossians 3:1,3. "Since, then, you have been raised *with Christ*,…For you died, and your life is now hidden *with Christ* in God" (emphasis added). If you're dead, how can you do anything? You can't. Who can? Jesus, the One who raised you to life! He is the giver of life and power, not you. It's not about you anymore, but about Him. Ultimate victory is not in our ability to walk, but in His strength.

Ugly Looking, Sweet Tasting Fruit

My family and I decided to plant a nectarine tree a few years ago. One year, the fruit had a rough yellowish exterior rather than a smooth reddish-orange skin. Some nectarines had deep grooves while others were covered in clear sticky sap! It was definitely a disappointment. The next year, we were cautiously optimistic about the coming harvest…until the fruit started growing. They just didn't look edible. In fact, they looked hideous. Our hopes were dashed. Then someone suggested, "Why don't you just let them ripen and see what happens?" With nothing to lose, we took their advice and left the fruit alone until harvest time.

Once we cut that first nectarine open, our fears washed away. It looked perfect inside – a soft, natural yellow. We trimmed off the ugly parts and sunk our teeth into one of the sweetest and juiciest nectarines we'd ever eaten. I was happier than I'd been since planting that tree as I munched on that delectable fruit.

Our Imperfections, Jesus' Perfection

We saw ugliness. God saw deliciousness. We see our imperfections. God sees our perfection because He sees Jesus, the Perfect One. We see ourselves as sinners. God sees us as saints (Philippians 1:1). As we walk with our God, we need to see ourselves as He does – already perfect. "When Christ, who is your life, appears, then you also will appear with Him in glory." It's a done deal! We're already at the top of the hill. It's only a matter of time. "We know that when He appears, we shall be like Him, for we shall see Him as He is. Everyone who has this hope in Him purifies himself, just as He is pure," (1 John 3:2-3). My friends, the top of the hill is a certainty because we're already in His hands. We are hidden in Jesus. The Father sees perfection when He sees us. Not because of anything we've done, but because of what Jesus already did at the cross.

That is something to rejoice about as we daily walk in the presence of our God. He sees us in a totally different way than we see ourselves. He sees the sweetness in our lives, even when we don't. He sees what we will become, even though we can't. We don't come to Him perfect. He makes us perfect after we come to Him (Hebrews 10:10). We don't have to live or act a certain way before we come to Christ. He's the one who changes us from the inside out to become more like Him.

See Others As Jesus Sees You

I walked to the top of the hill with my wife and daughter.

Could I have done it alone? Yes. Could I have made it up much faster by myself? Yes. Would it have been just as enjoyable? No. Together, we made it through the hard stretches and experienced the same sense of accomplishment. It wasn't about getting to the top; it was about the journey.

Your walk in the presence of God is not a solo experience. It was never designed to be that way. The moment we put our faith in Jesus as our Lord and Savior, we are not only made secure children of God, but we are also put into a family, one body (1 Corinthians 12:13). We were immersed ("baptized") into a group of people who are also walking in the presence of God.

You didn't come to God perfect, and neither did they. We are all sweet on the inside and a little deformed on the outside! God sees what we can become. Can we see each other the same way?

Walk With a Team

Romans 15:7 reminds us to accept one another as Christ has accepted us. Acceptance means that we see the imperfections, but that we let God bring out the sweetness. Jesus sees our hearts exactly as they are. What does He see? Perfection, and perfection in progress at the same time. It's through His grace and mercy that we're allowed into the warmth of the presence of God. We are to accept each other as we are – sweetness and ugliness alike.

Jesus certainly doesn't like everything we do. We will not like everything our fellow climbers do either. *Acceptance doesn't mean we have to call sin acceptable.* Instead, we are supposed to tell each other the truth in love (Ephesians 4:15). The context is so that "we will in all things grow up into Him who is the head, that is, Christ." We must be committed to walking in the truth of God's Word, not walking in our opinions, church traditions or Christian clichés.

We do our fellow climbers no good when we act as though what they're doing is okay when it's actually destroying their lives. The truth sets us free to experience the joys along the way and on top of the hill. In contrast, lies make us slide down the hill and hit the rocks along the way. Acceptance means that we are open to each other and our different levels of progress on the path.

Let the Spirit Help the Team

Having said that, does that mean we do nothing? No, what it does mean, however, is that it's the Spirit's job to convict people of their sin, not ours. He knows exactly what sin needs to be dealt with first. He sees their today and their tomorrow. He knows what to work on, and when to work on it. The Spirit, at times, will use fellow walkers to point out where the slippery, rocky soil is. He will use other believers to point out the lies in our thinking. Yet, this takes place in a loving "walk-with-you-through-it" relationship.

We are climbing the hill together. We are enjoying this personal walk in the presence of our God together. Thus, we are to nudge each other's thinking toward the truth of God's Word. The Spirit of God using the Word of God in the context of the people of God will get the job done of making that nectarine ripen to sweetness on the tree. The Spirit can use us to help each other examine what's going on in our heads. What is the lie that we're holding onto that says our current behavior will get us to the top of the hill? What lies are coming out of our mouths that we don't even realize we're saying? The Spirit of God will use fellow climbers to expose those lies and give each other the truths they need to replace those lies. We become a tool in the hands of a holy God to help His holy ones become more holy, closer to the flame. This takes tremendous amounts of love.

Colossians 3:12-14, "As God's chosen people, holy and dearly loved, clothe yourselves with compassion, kindness, humility, gentleness and patience. Bear with each other and forgive whatever grievances you may have against one another. Forgive as the Lord forgave you. And over all these virtues put on love, which binds them all together in perfect unity." Put simply, we need to accept one another where they're at, though not necessarily liking what they do, while lovingly nudging them toward Jesus.

Take the Next Step – View Yourself and Others Correctly

Are you a perfectionist? Learn to let it go! You didn't come to Jesus perfect. You came to Jesus to become perfected. Stop seeing yourself as worthless, because you're not! Jesus died to make you a secure child of God.

Life is about the climb with Jesus, not the aches and pains of the climb. Discouragement can set in if you only see your imperfections rather than your Jesus, who *will* make you perfect. Stopping your walk because you aren't this or that yet isn't worth it! Spend time each day rejoicing in what He has done, is doing and will do in your life. You *will* get to the top of the hill…someday.

This is true for individuals and for groups of believers. Make sure you are part of a group of believers that is willing to be real about their walk in the presence of God. Let your guard down with one or two people of the same gender, as you practice accepting one another where you're at, not necessarily liking what each other does, but lovingly nudging each other toward Jesus (see Appendix I – Walking with other believers).[1] If you don't know of a few people like this already (either within or outside your "church family"), ask the Spirit to lead you to them. Once He does, pray for Him to put it upon their hearts to form a group with you so you can hold each other accountable the process of becoming more like Jesus. Then get started on your climb together!

Are we there yet?
The cross was indeed up there!

Chapter 9

Is Your Love Cheap or Deep?

Use, don't abuse, God's grace and mercy.

The choices you make today determine your options tomorrow.

"In this way, love is made complete among us so that we will have confidence on the day of judgment, because in this world we are like Him. (1 John 4:17)

I was in Colorado for a family reunion. We were celebrating the grand moment when my brother and sister-in-law both turned 60 years old. Having arrived a few days early, I wanted to take advantage of one of the things the beautiful state of Colorado is known for – its outdoor activities. On the way to my mom's house, where I was staying, I saw a trailhead I thought would make for a great prayer walk, as it was surrounded by tall pine trees, a deep, blue sky and fresh mountain air. I told one of my nephews about it, who asked if he could go with me. We arranged a time to go hiking the next day.

Colorado Climbing Challenges

After meeting him at the parking lot, I tossed him a water bottle and off we went. The trail took us through all kinds of beautiful scenery on a steady incline. It wasn't an easy climb, by any stretch of the imagination, given the distance and elevation gain in thin mountain air. My nephew didn't let me go slow, either. We did stop along the trail to let faster hikers pass us, and I have to admit to using that trail etiquette to my advantage to catch my breath! Overall, though, we had a great time catching up and chatting about life as we followed the dirt path onward and upward.

Challenges Build Relationship

The hike was both long and tough for someone who had just arrived in the "Mile High State," but it was worth every step. This illustrates another important principle of walking in the presence of our God. *Our relationship with Him often develops through the uphill challenges.* In Romans 5:1-5, Paul describes an interesting progression of our faith lives, explaining, "We know that suffering produces perseverance; perseverance, character; and character, hope."

Our hope in Christ gets stronger in an interesting way – suffering. Real hope, the hope that gets us through painful situations, starts with suffering. Hard times should cause us to slow down and evaluate our lives, not get mad at God. We live in enemy-controlled territory; an overwhelming amount of the messages we receive are meant to drive us away from the only true source of joy and peace – Jesus. Challenges should draw us closer to Jesus, not drive us away. Challenges should make us ask, "Is my way of living giving me what I want and need out of life?" If not, these hard times will expose the weaknesses in the way we think and live. We can use these challenges, then, to allow Jesus to change us. If we're already living each day listening to and following Jesus, our sufferings will only affirm how we're approaching life.

Either by getting in line with or by keeping on in God's way of thinking and living, we must learn to persevere, which comes next in Romans 5. Each thought surrendered to Jesus or put to death changes our behavior. This brings on the next thing Paul talks about: character. The Spirit of God is making the great exchange – my temporary, unfulfilling character for His eternal, satisfying one. Instead of fighting the hard times, use them to become more like Jesus. When you do, you'll experience death on earth, and see life come out of it.

Eternal Hope Starts Today

This brings hope both now and forever! You can know from experience that He is real and that it's worth it to walk in His presence today. You can take God at His word. You can die to your own ways of handling challenges (i.e. taking your drug of choice), and put His truths into your head instead. You can act on those truths by faith in the Spirit's power and experience God changing your life. You can have peace in your heart, knowing you have a personal God whom you can trust while you're on this planet.

You've seen Him work in your past. And, as a result, you know He'll get you through your present, painful situation with a stronger faith and more Christ-like character than you had before. You know your faith works in the real world! This is hope based on fact, not fantasy.

When God changes your life He is essentially remodeling you into a new house that lasts for eternity. This gives a new perspective to challenges – they are actually good for us! They give us hope as we realize that our time on this planet is not wasted. As an illustration, imagine a house with a solid concrete foundation. That foundation is faith in Jesus, which makes you a child of God. With each challenge you face God burns off your character, the wooden studs of your house, through suffering. He replaces those old studs with new studs, Christ-like character, which lasts forever (1 Cor. 3:1-15). You're now victorious over the challenges and have become more like Jesus here on earth.

This is what John was talking about in 1 John 4:17. If we say we love Jesus, we will obey Him. As we do, our lives will be transformed with Christ-like character today, which will stand the fire test on Judgment Day when God will judge all believers based on how they lived on earth. When you live each day in the presence of God, your life will be changed. You will be more like Jesus, which will give you great confidence when you stand before the Judgment Seat of Christ (2 Corinthians 5:10). The Father will never reject Jesus. If He's seeing Jesus in you, what else can He do but smile?

Confidence Comes From the Hard Climbs

Like my Colorado climb, our walk in the presence of God will not be easy. Will the thin mountain air make you turn back, or will you keep going? This world will try to influence you to turn back and miss out on the opportunity to know and become more like Jesus. With each choice you make, then, you'll reveal how much you love Him. Is your love cheap, or deep? Will you only walk with Jesus when life is easy and full of blessing? Or, will you be like the prophet Habakkuk? He wrote, "Though the fig tree does not bud and there are no grapes on the vines, though the olive crop fails and the fields produce no food, though there are no sheep in the pen and no cattle in the stalls, yet I will rejoice in the LORD, I will be joyful in God my Savior. The Sovereign LORD is my strength; He makes my feet like the feet of a deer, He enables me to go on the heights," (Habakkuk 3:17-19).

Habakkuk knew about having a personal walk with his God in spite of his challenges. His love for God kept him walking in God's presence regardless of how tough life got. Though his farming career might have been ruined, and there might have been no crops to pay his bills, he kept on rejoicing in his Lord.

Habakkuk is the same author who penned the phrase that was foundational to the Protestant Reformation, "The righteous will live by his faith," (Habakkuk 2:4). He didn't make this statement in the oxygen-rich air of sea level, but in the thin air of the mountains on which he stood tall. He knew that God was still with him and this gave him tremendous security despite living in a very insecure situation.

The Smart Choice

Habakkuk learned something we also need to learn on our journey. *It isn't worth leaving God's presence, no matter how hard life gets.*[1] If we choose to turn our backs to Him by living our way, we choose to ignore His presence in our lives and the benefits that come with it. Though our careers may be spiraling downward and our bills spiraling upward, why would we want to ignore the only One who can bring us peace? Only by living in relationship with Him can we ever hope to pull out of the tailspin. The choices we make today affect our options tomorrow. If we choose to leave God's presence through sinning today, we choose the negative side effects of that choice tomorrow, such as feeling alone, ashamed, or angry.

What about God's grace? Won't I be forgiven? Yes, you will; but, you need to understand something about God's grace: It isn't cheap. God shows us this fact in the book of Leviticus with the various sacrifices (Leviticus 1-7). If you sinned intentionally and wanted to get back into God's presence, it cost the life of an animal (a burnt or "come near" offering). If you wanted peace with God again, it cost the life of an animal (a peace or "fellowship" offering). If you left God's presence unintentionally, an animal still had to die (a sin or "purification" offering). Gaining forgiveness and reentering the presence of God took time, effort and money. It was a hassle to leave God's presence, even more so if you had no animals to sacrifice or money to purchase them because your crops had failed.

The Ultimate Time to Keep Walking

In other words, a difficult period was not the time to even entertain the thought of leaving God's presence. It was time to trust Him even more because you knew it would cost you to be reconciled if you left! Yet, isn't this the time most believers think about leaving God's presence? *God, I can't handle this. Why are you letting this happen to me? Don't you care?* (We'll discuss this more in Chapter 10.)

He does care, and that is why He sent Jesus to die for us. We receive forgiveness and the ability to come into the presence of God through the life and death of Jesus. His sinless life insured that His blood would cleanse us from all unrighteousness – both intentional and unintentional. Grace is not cheap! It cost the Father a lot of time, effort, and the life of His Son, Jesus Christ. Please, don't begin to err in your thinking that God has lessened the hassle of His "return policy" by making it "easy" to return due to what Jesus did on your behalf. Jesus' coming to this earth, living perfectly, dying and rising to life was a huge hassle!

How dare we abuse it! How dare we say, "God will understand how much I hurt and why I need to leave His presence for a while to figure it out. He'll forgive me." *Yes, He is and will always be there to forgive and give you a hand up when you fall.* And He certainly understands your situation, more clearly than you do. He understands how much *your decision* to turn your back on Him will cause *you even more pain!* He also understands that this kind of attitude tramples on the One He loves – His Son, who did all the work so you could enter His presence; and the One you say you love – Jesus, who gave you every tool necessary to keep looking into the Father's loving eyes.

Our God knows that suffering is meant to bring us closer to Him, not push us away. He knows we'll find everything we need in His presence. He created this world to operate that way. He wants to draw us closer to Him so He can meet those needs. He further knows that for most of us it will take adversity to nudge us closer. Grace is not the liberty to do stupid things or to leave His presence with the expectation we'll be forgiven anyway. No, grace should be seen for what it is. It's the opportunity to walk in the presence of God today, even though we deserve complete separation from Him forever.

Take the Next Step – Rightly Use God's Grace

The price of admission to walk in the presence of God was extremely expensive. It cost the life, not of an animal, but of Jesus Himself. Jesus' death is the price God paid to provide forgiveness when you leave His presence. He wants you back that badly. When you leave His presence, it hurts you!

Use God's grace for what it is intended. Use it to draw closer to Jesus, to grow strong during tough times. Use it to gain confidence to live each day on this earth, and when you enter eternity. Ask yourself, "Is my love for Jesus deep or cheap?" Deep love will use God's grace correctly. Cheap love will abuse it. Here's a way to determine whether your love is deep or cheap: Think about a recent challenge you faced. Did this situation cause you to walk away, slow down, or draw closer to Jesus? If it was the former two, it's time to use the **FREEdom** principles (Appendix I – Transform your behavior by changing your thinking). Expose the lie behind your choice to abuse God's grace, exchange it with the truths Jesus gives you, and then practice using God's grace next time to stay in His presence.

Grace is an expression of God's love for you. Use it correctly to keep walking and talking with Jesus even when that walk is uphill in thin mountain air.

Chapter 10

Walk, Don't Dance with Jesus

Be you, but let Him.

"Not by might nor by power, but by My Spirit,' says the LORD Almighty."
(Zechariah 4:6)

I hate to admit it, but there are times I honestly don't want to walk with my God. There are times when I'm feeling insecure about life, usually on Mondays after the Sunday service or after I speak in front of a group. I may start having a beat-me-up session in my head over my defeats and failures to the point that I don't want to do anything on my to-do list, let alone the important things. This attitude leads to one of my drugs of choice – wasting time on low priority tasks. I call them "time-fillers." They fill my time until I get my head straight, which usually takes prayer. So, by not going on a prayer walk I'm avoiding the very Person who can help me get back on track! Additionally, time-fillers are usually things that can be done quickly, leaving me time to take other drugs of choice. This makes me feel even worse, allowing the beat-me-up session to last even longer.

Dancing with God

Not too long ago, the Spirit showed me why I took this "time-filler" drug." I call it, "dancing with God." Dancing with God is where I try to find a reason to either get mad at God or myself, which is my attempt to justify walking away from Him to take my drug of choice. I'll start getting close to God. Then I get mad at Him for not doing something I thought He should do (on my timetable, of course). I say or do something stupid, which I feel justifies my walking away from Him. Then I get mad at myself, and eventually come back to God. I do this "dance" repeatedly with God, but I'm always the one who loses.

That's what was happening when I didn't want to go on my prayer walk. I was dancing with God by focusing on the reasons I shouldn't take that prayer walk. The Spirit of God stepped in and got me out of the house and on the road to getting back into the presence of God, literally.

Walking Instead

In Psalm 13 David said, "How long must I wrestle with my thoughts and every day have sorrow in my heart? How long will my enemy triumph over me? But I will trust in Your unfailing love; my heart rejoices in Your salvation. I will sing to the LORD for He has been good to me," (13:2,5-6). I love David's honesty. Something was greatly troubling him and stealing his peace of mind, and I certainly could relate to that. That day, God brought David's solution back to my mind. Instead of focusing on his guilt, David spent time remembering how much his God loved Him. *He rejoiced in what God had already done for him and in him despite what was going on in his life.* If David could do that, so could I. And what better way to do it than to get out of the house and walk in the presence of my God outdoors.

I spent the next hour and a half walking. I followed the dirt roads winding around freshly tilled wheat fields, remembering all the good things God had done for me in the past. I remembered how much He loved me and wanted me around Him. I could finally sing songs to Him (even if my voice isn't that great), rejoicing over what He had done and would do again. By the time I got home, I was back in the presence of God, focused on Him and on doing what He wanted me to do – the higher priority items.

Experience God's Power to Keep Walking

Paul prays that the Ephesian believers would know "His incomparably great power for us who believe. That power is like the working of His mighty strength, which He exerted in Christ when He raised Him from the dead and seated Him at His right hand in the heavenly realms," (Ephesians 1:18-20).

God wants us to experience the same exact power that raised

Jesus from the grave. I was feeling dead inside before I went out on my prayer walk. I needed to feel alive again. *Okay God, You want me to know resurrection power in my everyday situations. How does that look?* I dove into Scripture to answer that question. What I found was surprising. It's my understanding that the power of God is seen when He does what only He can do. We often think of miracles and healings when it comes to God's power. That is part of it (Acts 6:8), but God's power was also seen when the apostles spoke with great boldness before the Israelite government (Acts 4:8,13). There was no outward miracle, other than an uncommon boldness. We see God's power as Stephen stayed supernaturally calm while being stoned to death (Acts 7:55). Elijah was able to run and keep ahead of Ahab, who rode in a chariot pulled by horses (1 Kings 18:46). All were instances of God doing something that these people couldn't do on their own. This is the power that comes from the Spirit of God, which sometimes doesn't seem very dramatic from a human point of view.

The power of God showed up in my life that day. The Spirit called to mind a verse I hadn't used in a while. The Spirit helped me remember how it went the last time I took my time-filler "drug." He also reminded me how good it felt to know that I've heard my God speak to me in the past.

It took the Spirit's power to help me understand and use my biblical tools (aka the *Set free Nowww* principles) to personally walk in the presence of God. I needed the Spirit's power to be able to filter out the lie-based messages in order to hear my Jesus. He helped me work through the sense of defeat and insecurity as I remembered God's love for me. He led me to rejoice over what Jesus would do in the future, despite the challenges I would face (external or self-inflicted).

God-Filtered Challenges

I want to talk about a well-worn phrase, "God never gives me more than I can handle." You might have even used it on yourself or with others. Stop and think about that statement. Put it through your biblical filter. Is it true or a lie? Let's walk through some biblical examples to find the answer.

If you read the book of Job, you see how Satan wanted to crush Job, but had to get permission from God before he could do anything (Job 1:6-12; 2:1-6). Jesus said in Matthew 24:22 that if the

Tribulation is not cut short during the end times, no one would survive, including believers. "But for the sake of the elect those days will be shortened." Though Satan has a free will, he must still check with God before he does anything. Our enemy would love to remove us from this planet before or when we come to faith in Jesus. He doesn't want any competition for people's souls! He certainly doesn't want us to live on earth and let Jesus shine through us (Matthew 5:13-16). So, the first part of "God never gives me more than I can handle" is true. Our sufferings, our challenges are filtered by our Father. He will never allow our enemy to overwhelm us.

The second part of the phrase, however, is a lie. Isn't handling life my way what gets me into trouble? I need more of the Spirit's help in challenging times, not more of me. 1 Corinthians 10:13 states, "God is faithful; He will not let you be tempted beyond what you can bear. But when you are tempted, *He will* also *provide a way* out so that you can stand up under it." What is that way? Himself! He wants to handle it through and for you. He wants to give you the strength to get out of the house to walk with Him instead of dancing with Him. He wants to bring back to your memory the principles of prior victories and defeat, so you keep walking in His presence.

God-Given Power to Overcome Challenges

In the last chapter we talked about Habakkuk being able to rejoice in spite of the fact that his career was going nowhere, and his bills were coming from everywhere. He did this by rejoicing in his Lord; he was joyful in God his Savior.

There is a saying I like to use, "There is only one person with an "S" on His chest and it ain't me or you!" You and I are not Superman; we can't save anyone else, let alone ourselves. Jesus is the Savior, the only Person with an "S" on His chest, and *the only* way of escape. He is the power behind the victory. When I didn't want to get out of the house and walk with my God it was the Spirit's power that got me going. His power did what I humanly couldn't do.

In 2 Corinthians 10:5 we are told to take prisoner "every pretension that sets itself up against the knowledge of God." One of these pretensions is the ego, or "I" problem. It's us saying we can handle life by ourselves. It's the belief that we can change our own lives and fix our own problems. The Bible challenges that belief, saying it is God's Spirit who will empower us to walk in the presence of our God.

God's Power Takes Different Forms

This power will not always look the same, which is part of the mystical side of our walk with Christ. Sometimes it might come with an obvious miracle or audible voice; sometimes it will be an intense emotional revelation. Sometimes it will just be the simple power to do what we can't do on our own. In my case, it meant getting out of the house to prayer walk in order to hear from Him instead of giving in to my own wants. This is as much the Spirit's power as a physical healing. In fact, we need to see more of this type of power that helps us make the (sometimes hard) choice to stay in His presence.

And please, do not overlook another very important conduit of the Spirit's power: other believers. Proverbs 27:6, "Wounds from a friend can be trusted, but an enemy multiplies kisses." Hebrews 3:13 states, "Encourage one another daily, as long as it is called Today, so that none of you may be hardened by sin's deceitfulness."

I am blessed to have such people around me who listen to and follow Jesus for themselves *and* for me. They notice if I'm telling lies to myself or to others, deliberately or accidentally. The Spirit allows them to see things in my life that I don't see on my own, which can be encouraging or, at times, quite painful! The question is, "Will we allow other believers to speak into our lives?" I do.

One Sunday after service, a trusted friend of mine came up to me with what they believed was an important spiritual message that the Lord wanted them to tell me (1 Corinthians 12:8). It was obvious that they were struggling to share it, though, since I was their pastor. (As a note, the specifics of what they shared are not as important as the fact that they dared to share it!) I carefully listened to them, thanked them, and then asked them to email me what they said so I could take it to the Lord. As believers, we are all in the process of learning how to better listen to Jesus, which makes it important to test information as we receive it. We do this through listening to Jesus in the Word, asking Him to confirm what is true and filtering out the rest.

As I went through the filtering process, I kept hearing one specific truth: "Be you, but let Him." This took me down a road I wouldn't have taken on my own! I needed to hear, in a fresh way, the truth that I am God's workmanship, created in Christ Jesus for the good works that He prepared me to do (Ephesians 2:10). God made me the way He did. He will use me the way He made me. *But it still has to be Him doing it, not me.* Anything I accomplish has to be through His power, not mine.

For example, God made me someone who gets excited about His Word, whether I'm speaking to a large group or having a one-on-one discussion. This passion shows through my voice and body language. Yet, it is not my voice or body language that will convince people to follow Jesus, or drive home the point He's trying to make. In the Bible, the Spirit used different people, who used different words and illustrations, to get His message down on paper. If I think my passionate way of communicating will convince people, the focus is on me and not on God. If, however, it's the Spirit expressing His passion through me, then the focus is on God.

God's Power, not Man's Wisdom

As I processed what my friend told me, I was reminded of what Paul said in 1 Corinthians 2:4-5. He explained, "My message didn't come with wise and persuasive words, but through a demonstration of the Spirit so that your faith will not rest upon man's wisdom, but God's power." Paul still gave the message the way only he could. Paul lived out his own words from Ephesians 2:10; he was God's workmanship, created in Christ Jesus for the good works which God had prepared for him to do. Still, it was the Spirit who worked through Paul to bring that message into people's hearts and bear fruit.

God made me passionate about following Him and sometimes I have to ask, "Am I manufacturing this passion or is the Spirit?" It's not always easy to discern, but the specific truth the Lord wanted me to hear is that *it has to be the Spirit, not me; only He can change lives.* God used the message from my friend to empower me to stay walking in His presence, despite my doubts and questions.

I wrote to my friend and shared what I heard the Lord say, especially the connection to 1 Corinthians 2:4-5. My friend wrote back the following. "NO WAY! That is awesome! You aren't going to believe me, but in my daily reading today was that verse! I was going to text you and then didn't as *I doubted if I was supposed to say something*. I just wrote it in my journal with a couple other things for myself. That is what I was trying to get at, freedom for you! It's His Spirit and power!…Watch what He will do as you surrender all to Him. What a beautiful thing if the people of the church would be who they were created to be and let the Holy Spirit do what He has already ordained for them to do! I guess it starts with us, being us in Jesus and showing people how the Lord uses individuals to show His love, power and glory. So cool!…"

Take the Next Step – Ask to Experience God's Power

You need God's power if you want to walk and not dance with Jesus. His power can come in a variety of ways, including through His people. It doesn't always come with bells and whistles, warm fuzzies, goose bumps, or the way you or others think it should. But *you will know* when He shows up!

Challenges are not optional – they're unavoidable. The question is, are you asking to know the power of the resurrection when they come? Or, are you just powering through your daily routine in the midst of them? If it's the former, are you expecting the Spirit to show up in certain ways; or, are you open to Him empowering you using other methods? Journaling can be a great tool here. Write out how the Spirit has empowered you in the past, focusing not on the method He used (as that can change), but on the fact that He did. This specific truth can help you stay in the presence of God rather than "dancing" with Him during your challenges.

If you're just going through your day in your own strength, I challenge you to ask the Spirit of God to empower you as only He can. (See Appendix I – *Walk with the Spirit*.) God wants you to know from experience how His power will get you through – not over or around – your challenges. To be you, the person God made you to be, you need the Spirit to empower you, so ask!

Chapter 11

Distractions Are Coming Your Way

Are you a picture-taker or a participant in life?

"Seek first His kingdom and His righteousness, and all these things will be given to you as well. Therefore do not worry about tomorrow, for tomorrow will worry about itself. Each day has enough trouble of its own." (Matthew 6:33-34)

*W*hat an awesome hike this is going to be. A group of us had tried the Lundy Canyon trail the year before, but we had started too late to finish it before dark. This year, though, we were determined to reach the top, wherever that was. I was excited about the day, especially because my entire family and a few friends were on the trail with me. I had a wonderful time in the Word before we left. On the drive to the trailhead at the northern end of Lundy Lake, I was doing what Psalm 30:4, said to do – "Sing to the LORD, you saints of His, praise His holy name." We all got our gear, took care of our last minute pit stops, and headed out.

Life's Distractions: Doubts

The trail took us first through a small grove of aspen and pine trees where we noticed tree stumps gnawed by beavers. Higher up we saw majestic waterfalls spilling over rocks, forming streams that fed blue-green lakes made by the beaver dams.

Then the first of many distractions hit. There I was, enjoying my walk in the presence of my God, viewing His creation of deep blue skies and intricate, purple flowers growing between rocks along the trail...when my wife asked, "Did you lock the car?"

I had our van key in my pocket. I had locked the van after everyone finished getting his/her gear. Then someone had to go retrieve another item, and I had unlocked the car. At this point, we probably had already gone about ¾ of a mile. I really didn't want to turn around and go check to make sure, but I couldn't remember hearing the horn that showed that the car had been relocked. I remembered hitting the lock button, but was it really locked?

This thought gnawed on me for a while, which meant I missed some of the beauty around me. Eventually I picked up my biblical **FREE**dom tools (see page 118), filtered the situation through the truths of God's Word and got back to enjoying my walk with Jesus. I began to notice the scenery along the trail again. At one point, it was lined with green ferns and deep orange Indian Paintbrush flowers growing alongside another type of purple flower (which made me wish for a nature book!) Then another distraction hit. *Which way do we go?*

Life's Distractions: Detours

We had come to a part of the trail that ran along a dry creek bed. The trail seemed to go through the creek bed, but that didn't seem right. My son and his friend walked a while up what they thought was the trail, only to return. That wasn't the direction. Did I stop and ask the Lord where we should go? Nope. I just kept scanning the area looking for the trail. After milling around for what seemed like forever (but was only about 5 minutes) we finally saw it. The trail crossed a log! After berating myself for a few moments, I once again filtered the situation using my biblical tools and got back into my God's presence again, able to enjoy Him and His creation.

In ten minutes we came to another beautiful waterfall, and were excited to find that we could climb up to it instead of admiring it from a distance. The sound of the rushing water below our feet almost drowned out our voices. The spray at the falls edge, combined with the shade of the trees, tamed the trail's heat. We dropped our packs happily, took photos from our picturesque overlook of the valley, and had a snack.

Life's Distractions: Discouragement and Disappointment

After this refreshing break, we continued onward and upward...until we came to what looked like a landslide! It seemed like the end of the trail. Then we were relieved to discover a series of switchbacks on the trail, and we followed those until there simply wasn't any more trail to follow. The only way to continue was to pick our way over the rock landslide.

As we slowly went on, slipping and sliding and crawling on our hands and feet, I knew we were done. I could see it on my wife's face. We'd left our map of the area's trails at the cabin. If there was a trail to be found, we couldn't see it. *Why didn't I bring the map? What if we don't accomplish my goal of getting to the top? Did I really come all this way for nothing!?*

Nothing? Could I really say that? Isn't this life about being with Jesus and enjoying Him as we walk through each day, no matter what happens? Isn't this life about allowing others to see Jesus in us and hopefully want a relationship with Him as well? Was this trip really only about getting to the top? Again, I had to filter the situation through God's Word.

Our kids and their friend started making their own trail as they went up the 45-degree incline. Meanwhile, my wife and I walked around a corner of this rocky hill and took in a wondrous view – another giant, cascading, rainbow-producing waterfall. We took off our climbing packs and savored the sights while munching on some beef jerky and gulping down water. Then we climbed down to a lower stream to check for any old mines from a bygone era.

The kids finally came down and we all went home with some great memories and pictures, plus a lesson for this book. Life happens. Distractions and disappointments will come your way and will attempt to draw you out of the presence of your God. Will you let them, or will you filter them out using your biblical tools?

Look Deep Into His Eyes

The author of Hebrews gives us an important principle that will help us stay in the presence of our great and awesome God. "Let us fix our eyes on Jesus, the author and perfecter of our faith," (Hebrews 12:2). The word for "fix" literally means to stare at in order to not just see the object, but to experience it. In Matthew 24:6 Jesus says, "You will hear of wars and rumors of wars, but *see* to it that you are not alarmed."

You can choose to focus on the distractions – the missed trail markers, missed goals, and problems – or on Jesus. Look at what happens when you focus on Him, while you walk the trails of life.

"*Your love*, O LORD, reaches to the heavens, *Your faithfulness* to the skies, *Your righteousness* is like the mighty mountains, *Your justice* like the great deep. O LORD, *You preserve* both man and beast. How priceless is *Your unfailing love*! Both high and low among men find refuge in the shadow of Your wings. They feast on the abundance of *Your house*; You give them drink from the river of delights." (Psalm 36:5-8, emphasis added)

I love this piece of Scripture, because I've experienced it while out walking – those deep blue skies, stunning mountains, the sight of birds hovering, and rushing waters. And they all point me back to my heavenly Father.

Are you doubting yourself and your abilities? This is a distraction. It will melt away as you keep walking in God's presence. Are you feeling unloved? Distraction. In your Father's presence is unconditional love. Are you facing discouragement and disappointment? Distraction. Your God is leading you into victory. Are you feeling let down by others? Distraction. Jesus is faithful – stay focused on Him. Does life seem unfair? Distraction. Justice radiates from your God. Does tomorrow seem uncertain? Distraction. Jesus is already there and will walk with you. Are you afraid? Distraction. Your God is a place to hide and feel safe.

Take the Next Step – Keep Listening Despite the Distractions

God promises a river of delights to those who stay in His presence. Satan doesn't want you to experience them, so expect distractions. You don't have to let him take you out of God's presence! Use your biblical tools to filter life's distractions out so you can keep listening to Jesus.

This is another good time to journal, on paper or electronically. What distractions has your enemy successfully used in your past? Those distractions will likely come again, so be ready to defeat them! Use the specific truths you've stored in your shield of faith while listening to Jesus. It's this shield that will help you stay focused on Jesus and experience Him in all circumstances. It's this shield that will help you enjoy the good things God has for you. (If you're not regularly reading your Bible, re-read the previous sentences.)

Life on this planet is not about reaching some destination. It's about walking in Jesus' presence, despite life's distractions. You're on a trail with Jesus that will allow you to take in some beautiful sights. Enjoy the walk!

What an awesome hike this is going to be.
My family is posing at the waterfall where we stopped for a snack.

Chapter 12

Stick to the Path!

Switchbacks are your friends.

"I am the Way." – Jesus (John 14:6)

M y wife and I have been enjoying the use of a cabin near Mammoth Lakes for over 15 years, sometimes with family, sometimes just the two of us. We love its secluded location and hearing Laurel Creek break along both sides of the cabin. There's a nearby meadow where cattle meander during the spring, and there are beautiful mountain colors throughout the year to enjoy.

Behind this cabin is a trail that goes up to Laurel Lake, the source of the creek. We looked at the numbers for this trail – there was a 2,000 foot elevation gain over the 4.5 mile length. My wife, Jan, and I decided to attempt it on the second day of our vacation. We had acclimated ourselves the day before by taking an easy 5 mile walk from our cabin down a gravel road, along a tree-lined creek to a cattle waterhole, and then back.

We knew this particular hike would be mostly straight up. There were switchbacks – long, zigzag trails up the mountainside – but there were also shorter alternatives. In fact, our hiking map stated that this trail was actually a 4-wheel-drive road for the first half of the climb. With that in mind, we tried to save ourselves some time and elevation and avoid "needless" switchbacks by starting out from our cabin, rather than walk the quarter of a mile to the trailhead.

Mistake #1: Making Our Own Path

We followed Laurel Creek from where it split behind our cabin to a spot where we thought we could pick up the trail. It was a slightly overcast day, which made for beautiful hiking weather. We had our hiking packs full of snacks and water. The dirt was soft as we picked our way through some low-lying brush. At times we even followed tracks up the hill, the animal droppings leaving no doubt as to what had walked there before us.

We were making steady progress up the hill when we noticed our first obstacle – an embankment that had been invisible from the bottom of the hill. No hiking trail. We stopped, looked at each other, and decided on a new course of action, which was to follow an animal trail over a series of rock patches. Animals are more sure footed than we were, even with our good hiking boots; I think I twisted my ankle a few times as we picked our way through the maze of rocks.

After about another half mile, we finally hit the trail. We climbed and we climbed and we climbed. There were some small (very small) stretches where the trail was level, but for the most part all we did was climb up. On the bright side, we could see the creek from the trail. We even spotted a small herd of black cattle grazing in the pastures around the creek. The path they took up the hill looked much easier than ours.

As we continued up the Laurel Lake trail a light breeze started. We are fairly experienced hikers and were prepared for all types of weather, but didn't want to stop at that point to put on our rain/wind ponchos. We had worked up a good sweat at this point and continued climbing. It seemed that the Laurel Creek to our right just kept going and going. *The lake has to be up there somewhere. How about here? Nope, not yet – let's keep climbing.*

Mistake #2: Focusing on Our Fatigue

Then we saw them. Switchbacks. If we wanted to get to the top we only had one choice: take those switchbacks. As we started on this tedious part of the trail, we both noticed that there appeared to be another trail heading toward the creek and up the hill to where we thought the lake must be. We both made a mental note of this trail as we continued our attack on "The Beast," which was what we were beginning to call this portion of the climb.

Then Jan made an interesting observation. "It didn't really dawn on me until now. This hike is not just 4.5 miles. I knew I could handle that before we started. But it's actually 9 miles round trip! I have to come back down these switchbacks!" She wasn't saying she wanted to turn around – she was just as determined as I was about finishing something we started. She was simply making a mental note of her current energy levels, how long it had taken us to get to this point, which was 3.5 miles of the supposedly 4.5 miles, and the amount of energy she would need to get down once we'd reach the lake. We kept climbing and eventually got out of the switchback section and saw that "The Beast" now went straight up. Was there really a lake up here?

I saw the look on her face as her pace was beginning to slow and the stops were a little more frequent. In what I thought would be an encouraging statement I said, "I'll just walk on ahead quickly to see how close we are to the lake." The moment I said "quickly," however, I realized I had made a mistake. *Uh oh, did that sound condescending?* I never looked back to find out. I just kept going.

There is a Lake After All!

I was totally relieved once I got to the top of this ridge. The lake was real, and I was staring at it…down the hill from where I was standing. In the meantime, it started to rain, and this time I did put on my rain poncho. I called Jan to tell her the good news that Laurel Lake was within sight. I did, however, wait to tell her that she would have to walk down the path to get to it. We'd make that decision once we were standing next to each other.

The rain slowly began to subside as I saw her dark blue poncho-covered head appear. She brightened up a little as she saw me. (I don't know whether it was because she was happy to see me, or the fact that she had finally gotten to the top.) Then her face changed. She saw the lake below. She looked at me. She looked at it. I told her that we made it to the top, and that we didn't have to actually go to the lake unless we wanted to. We could sit here and enjoy the beauty of the scenery *below* us while we had a bite to eat and recovered for the walk back down.

Not surprisingly, she informed me that we were going to that lake. I smiled, and after a brief rest we finished the "uphill" portion of this hike by going down to the lake. It was a gorgeous sight too…and then we saw a Jeep coming up from the lake! I knew the thought going through both our minds. *Wouldn't it be nice to hitch a ride back?* We didn't say a word to the people in the Jeep, though, or to each other. We simply kept walking.

Finally we made it! The lake was a beautiful rippling green since the clouds were blocking out the sky and sun. We sat on a little land mass protruding into the water as we ate, though it was well past lunchtime by then. As we were resting, we made the mistake of looking at the walking app on my phone. Much to Jan's horror, the hike up wasn't 4.5 miles. It was 5.36 miles! Not only had we gone almost a mile longer than anticipated, but that also meant the round trip mileage would mean almost 11 miles, not 9!

Mistake #3: Trusting Our Eyes

Uphill out of the lake. Downhill through rock covered switchbacks. And 5.36 more miles before we'd be safely back at our cabin. Jan told me, in a way that only she can, "I'm not going back uphill to go down those switchbacks. Remember that trail we saw that led up here? Let's take it." I thought about it, then said, "Let's do it."

After packing up our lunch we found the "trail" and started home. We reached the lower Laurel Lake easily. Seeing what looked like the continuation of the trail, we stayed to the right of the lake, but it turned out to be an animal trail, not a human one. We kept on going, still pleased with our shortcut. This good feeling – and the trail – lasted about 15 minutes. Soon we could hear the creek, but couldn't see it because of all the ground cover. There was also no trail visible ahead, only tightly crowded aspen trees. They were beautiful because the fall color show was about to begin. We weren't thinking about that at the moment, though; we were tired and just wanted to get home.

We twisted our bodies in so many different ways to get through this grove of trees I think we could have made any gymnastics team! As usual, we were wearing shorts, and our legs kept getting scratched with every new direction we took. I fell on my rear end going down hill and stopped when my back hit a tree. I twisted my ankle on a branch and fell again. I wasn't lost. I knew we'd eventually hit the trail, I just couldn't see it through the trees!

Better Decisions

I kept getting frustrated, and then getting under control again. I knew that a calm person makes better decisions than a person who's upset. I'd send up a prayer now and then, but I was distracted by the brush and all those aspens we needed to get through. *How in the world do the animals get through all this? Wasn't that an animal trail we started on?* Sometimes I'm a very slow learner. The animal trail on the uphill portion of this journey took us through rocky patches; the animal trail was taking me through a forest on the way down.

On and on we went. From time to time, we'd cross a creek or a dry creek bed. What was worse, getting our legs scratched, or getting our feet wet? We held a conference in the middle of the "forest" and decided to follow the creek. God must have put that thought into our heads because we barely got our feet wet when, within minutes, we were facing a very level, brownish yellow, clear open space meadow. We were out of the trees and on our way home! Within about another 15 minutes we were back on the trail, the real trail that came out of the switchback section.

Mistake #4: Making Our Own Path – Part 2

While better than the animal trail, this trail was made for 4-wheel drive vehicles, not for people. There were rocks embedded in it all the way down. Do you know how uncomfortable it is to walk on rocks when you've already walked uphill 5.36 miles, fought through underbrush downhill and are feeling nearly exhausted? And, no matter how careful we were to avoid those rocks (which was both time consuming and tiring) we still stepped on them!

We finally came around a bend in the trail and could see the starting point of this grand adventure, where we both wanted so very badly to be at this point. As we came around this bend, lo and behold, there was another set of switchbacks! We didn't see them before, as we had taken the scenic creek route up.

We looked at each other. We could make a straight line to the cabin, but it would mean leaving the trail and bypassing the switchbacks. This new "path" would certainly save us time. Our feet were tired. We were tired. *Straight line here, we come!*

I don't like to harm wildlife or step on plants so I tried to pick a path along the dirt sections in between them. I was doing a great job until the dirt path disappeared! Our legs got scratched all over again. One particular path led to an area full of boulders; it was there that I broke my trekking pole and had another fall. Covered in dirt, I shook my head – we should have stayed on the path. Switchbacks are indeed our friends. We did eventually make it home and had a good laugh about it…much, much later.

Jesus Blazed *The* Trail

The principle should be obvious by now. Stay on the path. Switchbacks are your friends! Jesus calls Himself "the Way" in John 14:6 for a reason. He looked at the hill called life and blazed the only trail to the top, even though it isn't always the easiest. He showed us how to listen to and follow His Father at all times (John 5:19; 8:28; 12:30). He is our example of how to personally walk in the presence of our God. He lived a sinless life to show us how to do it. When life gets hectic and we feel the pressure, we take our drug of choice. We think, "Sin now, and our life will be better." We decide getting off the path is easier and better. We can't see ahead to know that it will scratch our legs, twist our ankles, and cover us in dirt as we fall.

It's all too easy to give into the building pressure rather than stay in God's presence. Or maybe we've experienced victory in one area of our lives, only to become discouraged when we find Satan attacking in another. In contrast, Jesus never sinned in *any* area of His life. The pressure He felt never lessened – it only increased! He chose to stay on the path His Father laid out for Him, even though they both knew it was leading Him to the greatest pressure point in history – the beatings, the cross, and, ultimately, separation from each other. This pressure built up so much that Jesus sweat blood. Yet He never chose to meet His needs His way. He never chose to take the easy way out by getting off the path. He never sinned. He walked the switchbacks.

Yes, going uphill is hard. Yes, switchbacks are tough. Yes, there will be rocks to avoid on the trail. But you have a choice. You can trust Jesus that the trail He made for you is best – or, you can choose to leave the path and end up covered in bruises and dirt.

Take the Next Step – Stay on the Path

Jesus said that following Him will set us free from the negative things that our way of living brings. His way brings peace, joy, and love. It brings a reason to get out of bed in the morning. It brings satisfaction, fulfillment, and self-control.

Now is a good time to again ask yourself whether the paths you've taken have brought you what you wanted in life. What tactics does your enemy use to get you to stop following Jesus? Trusting your senses? Leaning on your own reasoning? Relying on your emotions? Taking the easy way out? Avoiding the switchbacks? Complaining about your life?

Use your biblical tools to filter out these lie-based messages in order to hear the voice of Jesus. He says, "Come to Me, all you who are weary and burdened, and I will give you rest. Take My yoke upon you and learn from Me, for I am gentle and humble in heart, and you will find rest for your souls. For My yoke is easy and My burden is light," (Matthew 11:28-30). You may be burdened by the consequences of your actions, by your choice of paths. Your Father offers a lake and a place to rest. He offers you His yoke – His path. He offers rest for your soul, even if your body still aches and life is still hard. With every decision throughout your day, keep asking the Spirit to empower you to pick up your biblical tools. This will give you the ability to listen to Jesus, so you can stay on the right path.

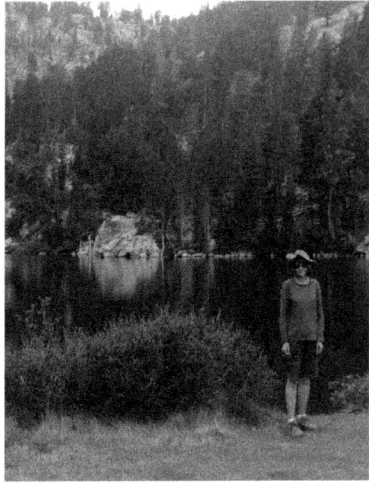

The lake has to be up there somewhere.

Chapter 13

Give Dad the Bag

Practice equals preparation.

"How priceless is Your unfailing love! Both high and low among men find refuge in the shadow of Your wings." (Psalm 36:7)

"Daddy, can I go with you?" asked my three and a half year-old son. I had been going on backpacking trips into the Sierras for the last couple of years with a buddy of mine when my son asked that question. I loved the idea, but I had to prepare him for the trip.

At this point in his young life, he liked me to carry him around in my arms or on my shoulders, which I enjoyed too. I'm a child of God who happens to be a dad myself. I've relished every stage of being a dad, and this was no different.

It's a Deal, Dad!

I knew, however, that if he wanted to go with me he had to be prepared to walk on his own while carrying a few things in his little backpack. I told him, "Doug, if you want to go with Daddy, you're going to have to practice walking for the next three months. Even though I love holding you in my arms, I'll have to carry our gear when we go backpacking. Understand?"

"Yes, Daddy."

"I'll be more than glad to take you if you can do that. Deal?"

"It's a deal, Dad."

From that point on, unless he was extremely tired, he walked everywhere we went. I even had him wear his little pack containing a few items. Of course, I was planning to carry all the necessary camping items in my pack: our sleeping bags, tent, cooking supplies, food, and water. With anything beyond a few clothes and toys, his pack would just be too heavy for him to carry on his own. He wouldn't make it up the three-mile trail to our campsite if he had to carry all the gear he'd need for the four days of camping!

Challenges and Triumphs

Doug was ready when hike day came. The elevation gain was less than 1,000 feet, but it took us through some beautiful scenery. This particular backpacking trip had a few firsts in store. The biggest one was that my son was coming with me. The other one was that it had been a rather wet year, and there were still patches of snow along our trail through the High Sierras. Normally some snow would be fine, but for a little boy with small legs it made for a couple of challenges. The first challenge was that the creeks were higher than normal, which made crossing them a little more difficult. He was a trooper, though. He crossed each creek by holding my hand and putting his feet right where I put mine.

Then came the second challenge. All that water was home to mosquitoes that must have seemed the size of baseballs to him. Doug wore a French Foreign Legion hat that covered his neck, and I made sure he wore plenty of bug repellent, but he still got bitten. I was very proud of my son that day. (I still am today!) He was like a little mountain goat as he kept on climbing. He didn't complain about the mosquitoes even as they buzzed around us. Step by step, he kept marching on until we finally made it to base camp, which was by a lake still partially covered with snow and ice. He had carried his little pack all by himself all the way up the trail, and beamed with pride when he finally got to take it off at the campsite. We had a great time on that trip. I'm not sure how much of it he remembers, but I will never forget it.

Let Dad Carry What Only He Can

This walk emphasizes an important principle of personally walking in the presence of God: Let your Father carry what only He can. Just walk with Him. You're not going to understand the "why" of every path He chooses for you, the load you might have to carry, or the challenges you might face along the way. Will you continue to trust your Father and keep walking, or will you give up and return home?

In Leviticus 19, God told the Israelites they were not to interbreed two different animals, plant two different crops in the same field, or wear clothes with two different types of threads. Technically, there was nothing sinful or abnormal about any of these plants or animals, but God never gave the Israelites a specific reason for any of these commands. What mattered was their obedience. If indeed He was the Lord their God, they would trust Him.

Jesus says the same exact thing to you and me in John 14:15, "If you love Me, you will obey what I command." As we listen to Jesus every day we won't understand all the reasons for what He's asking us to do. The question is, will we still follow Him anyway? He is asking us to trust Him, just like I asked my son to trust me when I said he had to walk on his own before he could go backpacking with me. When he asked why, I told him that I would be carrying all the gear and couldn't carry him too. Now, to the mind of a three-and-a-half-year-old, that still might not have made sense. To him, I was Dad; I could do anything. (Oh, how the teenage years would quickly dispel that notion!) Why couldn't I carry him and all the gear as well? I didn't explain all my reasons to him then, though. I just told him that he would have to trust me, which he did.

Trust Your Father

Like mosquitoes, our doubts, unanswered questions, and hurts can make our walks difficult. "God, I don't understand why this is happening to me?" "God, why are you not answering me?" "God, that person is being such a jerk. Why are you asking me to love them?" "God, you want me to forgive her for what she did to me. Are you kidding?" All the while, you're letting "mosquitoes" rob you of the joy of the hike. My son didn't want to wear the smelly, greasy bug repellent, but he did it anyway. Why? He trusted me. (Wearing the hat, however, was no problem – he thought it was cool.)

I read a story once about a little girl traveling with her father, a doctor, on a train. While sitting next to him, playing with her doll, she asked, "Where do babies come from?" He said nothing, and she didn't repeat her question.

When they reached their destination, her father asked her to pick up his medical bag. Try as she might, it was just too heavy for her small arms to lift. Seeing this, he picked it up while remaining silent. Once they reached the train platform he said, "My darling, the answer to your question is like my medical bag. It's too heavy for you to lift right now. One day, you will be strong enough to lift it. I'll give you the answer then. Do you trust me?" She nodded as they continued to walk, she with her dolly in hand and he with his medical bag.

Stress, a peace destroyer, shows up in situations that we find difficult to handle. If we focus on the stressful situation, we're more apt to use our drug of choice to (temporarily) relieve that stress. My son could carry his little pack with a few clothes and toys. If he had to carry all his gear, he would have never made it out of the car, let alone up to our camping spot. He simply was not physically capable of carrying a heavier load at that point in his young life. He let me carry what he couldn't so he could enjoy the hike and the camping.

Take the Next Step – Give Your Father Your Bags

You live in enemy territory where Satan wants to lay heavy loads, including the unanswered "whys," on your shoulders. Will you try to carry these loads yourself? Or, will you let your Father carry them while you walk in His presence?

Choose to give your bags to your Father by taking the following steps: Use the **FREE**dom process. Name the specific stressors, doubts, fears, hurts, questions, insecurities, and other issues that are too heavy for you to carry. Ask Jesus to expose the lies that make you think you have to carry them yourself. Exchange those lies for the specific truths He gives. Give those bags to Jesus – visualize Him taking them out of your hands. Then ask the Spirit for the strength to start focusing on what He's asking you to do at the moment. As you do, you'll find peace, even if you still don't have all the answers.

By using your *Set free Nowww* tools today, you'll be prepared for anything coming your way tomorrow…including baseball-sized mosquitoes. As new challenges come your way, you'll already be trained to stay focused on the truths that bring peace. You'll be used to filtering out the lies and thoughts that weigh you down. You'll be able to weather any storm that comes since you'll already be under the shadow of His wings (Psalm 91). If He really is your

God, trust Him. If you love Him, keep walking with Him even when life doesn't make sense to you. It does to Him, so let Him carry the weight.

Chapter 14

Making it Personal

Walking with Christ is an exercise of the willing.

Freedom in the hands of another is not freedom.

"We are the temple of the living God. As God has said: 'I will live with them and walk among them, and I will be their God, and they will be My people.'"
(2 Corinthians 6:16b)

As I look back over the chapters in this book, I see a lot of walks. I've walked every step in my cross-training shoes or hiking boots, and learned quite a few lessons. These lessons are not theoretical, but are very real and practical in the world in which we live. Like a friend of mine once said, "Walking with Christ is an exercise of the willing." No one can make you walk in the presence of God, or do it for you. It's my hope that these stories show you how God invites us to walk in His presence and makes even the hardest hills worth it.

Experience it for Yourself

One day the owner of a solar panel company gathered together 1,000 people to train them in solar energy. He taught them how the system worked, the benefits of solar energy, and how to sell solar panels to customers. After the training sessions concluded, he sent them off to sell solar energy. Instead of the success he expected, the sales were dismally low. His salespeople started to quit, and moved on to better jobs; they just couldn't get enough people to buy the panels. The product was good, but somehow that wasn't enough for people to purchase it.

With his company heading in a downward spiral and his stress levels going in the opposite direction, he decided to install solar panels on the roof of his own house. (Why he hadn't thought of doing this before is beside the point.) After a few months with the panels in full operation, he saw his electric bills drastically reduced! He was elated at being able to help both the environment and his pocket book. He not only saved money on his electric bills, but was also able to purchase items his family could never have afforded before. His family loved the extra money, and felt good about making less of an impact on the planet. The stress that had been a drain on them all began to let up.

His neighbors saw him put the solar panels on his roof, but it was when they saw him relaxed and getting more out of life that they asked him what was going on. He told them about how solar power worked and the benefits of installing it on his house. They couldn't argue with what they were seeing, and some of them installed solar panels on their roofs as well. Soon they started seeing savings of their own, as well as feeling proud about helping the environment. Not surprisingly, his company became profitable as more and more solar units were sold. The constant employee turnover stopped, and his company grew. It was a win-win situation.

Reap the Benefits for Yourself

I'm like that solar panel company owner. I'm personally reaping the benefits of walking in the presence of *my* God. I've experienced the peace and joy that comes from knowing my God in a very personal way. I know for a fact that *my* God is real and wants a relationship with me. I know from daily experience that *my* God talks to and walks with me. I know in my head *and* my heart that His Word is true and works in the everyday world in which I live. This shouldn't be a surprise; this is how He created the world to work.

Whether my fellow family members (believers in Jesus) or my neighbors (those who have yet to put their faith in Jesus) want to walk with Jesus or not, doesn't hurt my own walk. I'm experiencing Jesus in ways I haven't before and I love it! My faith is stronger and I have memories of how good my God is and how good it is to walk in the presence of my God, even when life doesn't make sense.

Don't get me wrong. I hope you'll pick up your biblical tools in the Spirit's power to do the same. I pray that my fellow believers will want to personally walk in the presence of their God. I pray that my "neighbors" will one day put their faith in what Jesus did and will do in and for them. He wants to walk with them as well.

I'm enjoying the kind of life that only comes by placing my freedom in God's hands. Freedom in the hands of another human is not freedom. If my joy, my fulfillment, and my security are dependent on anyone (including myself) other than Jesus, I'm in trouble. He came to give me freedom (John 8:32-32), joy (John 15:11), and life to the fullest (John 10:10).

It's hard to see anyone waste so much time and effort on a life that doesn't work. However, it's not my job to convince others of how wrong they may be or how good Jesus is. That's the job of the Holy Spirit. My job is to enjoy the low "bills" and to be ready to share with others when they want to listen. Once their worldview stops working, and they realize it, hopefully I will have shown them that there's a better alternative out there.

Mature Faith is More than Knowing About Jesus

I've come across so many believers who don't actually have a personal walk with the God they say they love. It's like they're trying to sell a product they've read about but have never tried. They act as if whoever has the most Bible knowledge wins; they've been taught to believe that having more Bible knowledge is equivalent to a mature faith when that isn't true. Hebrews 5:11-6:3 describes a person with mature faith as someone who *knows* the truth and can *use* it to process out the lies, discerning between good and evil. This person can then put this truth into action through the Spirit's power. When it comes to knowledge and faith, it's not either/or, but both/and.

The Bible often talks about gaining knowledge, understanding, *and* wisdom (Proverbs 2:1-8). We need to study and know the truths of Scripture. This is undeniable. Yet, many people stop there. They've bought the lie that *knowledge by itself equates to Christian maturity*. In reality, believers are meant to move beyond head knowledge to life change. For example, life change happens when we understand what the truth in a particular Bible passage is and then actually apply that truth in everyday life. Life change only comes when all the elements are in operation: knowledge, understanding, and wisdom-based action steps. As this happens, you will actually have good news to share with your family and neighbors – Jesus makes a difference!

Take the Next Step – Get Personal with Your God

Ask yourself, "Am I like the solar panel owner before or after he installed the panels on his own house?"

If your answer is, "Before," today is the day to choose to move beyond mere head knowledge to actually walking in the presence of God. It's time to start experiencing the benefits of walking with Jesus in your present reality, and not just talking about them.

If your answer is, "After," keep walking in the presence of your God! Keep showing Jesus while being ready to share why you're reaping all those benefits (1 Peter 3:15). Those around you may not come to faith in Jesus, but they won't be able to deny that faith in Him works in the real, everyday world. Think of how the world would change if every believer in Jesus actually walked with Him!

Chapter 15

The Decision to Walk

"Nothing changes until something changes." Anonymous

"Abram was ninety-nine years old, the LORD appeared to him and said, 'I am God Almighty; walk before Me and be blameless.'" (Genesis 17:1)

"Choose for yourselves this day whom you will serve.... But as for me and my household, we will serve the Lord." (Joshua 24:15)

If we want to become more like Jesus, something has to change – our thinking. If we continue to live by the same old thinking, we will end up living with the same old results, the sin-confession-sin cycle. We'll continue to repeat the same behaviors, causing us to reap the same results of frustration, disappointment, and disillusion. Then we'll keep confessing them to Jesus, and eventually falling into the same old sins again.

The Lesson of the Coins

I want to share with you a walking story I call "The Tale of Two Coins." There is a path that I often walk on near my home. I know its distance, and how long it will take to cover that distance. Knowing this, I can plan my daily schedule, which is a good thing. It also keeps me in control, which is not such a good thing. Routines keep me in charge, which means I don't feel like I need God.

Over the last few years, the Lord has been trying to teach me to keep my to-do list in His hands. He wants me to ask Him what should be next on the list, rather than just choose what I want done. The Lord emphasized that point on this particular walk. As I headed out on this day's prayer walk, I sensed the Lord telling me to walk my neighborhood. It was something I hadn't done for quite a while, and I knew it wouldn't take too long since I live on a short street with only two entrances/exits. After walking about half way, I came across two scuffed up pennies. Now, you can't buy much with two pennies, but those two have become very valuable to me because of what they represent.

I seem to "find" coins on my walks at just the right time. Each US coin has the phrase, "In God We Trust," stamped on it. When I start to doubt God's direction in my life this little phrase reminds me to ask myself the question, "Am I really trusting God?" This phrase helps me to remember the truth that just as He's taken care of me so far, He will continue doing so in the future. Over the years I have filled a half-gallon Mason jar in my bedroom with coins (there are some bills as well!) that I've picked up on my various walks. Picking up these coins has been just one way God encourages me to continue to trust Him.

Encouragement to Keep Walking

I had been feeling a little uneasy about the future before leaving on this particular walk. Would I seek to stay in my comfort zone and take my usual path, or would I leave that sense of control and be willing to go another direction – His? Well, I had already chosen to continue to walk in His presence and finding those pennies was His way of encouraging me to keep going. He didn't stop encouraging me when I left my street either. As I exited my housing tract, God led me to take another route I normally don't go, making a left here, a right there, all through the rolling hills around my house. This guiding kept going on mile after mile until I finally came to a junction where I normally would head home along a quiet dirt path.

This time, however, I sensed Him wanting me to continue to walk further from home by taking a surface street toward a busy state highway. I wouldn't usually walk on that sort of road, since I like to avoid the distractions of engines roaring and cars swooshing past me. "Seriously, Lord," I said silently. "You know how I avoid these streets. It's really hard to hear You there; You know all the distractions I'll face." This conversation didn't last long, though. I knew I was supposed to take the busy city street instead of the quiet farmland road. So off I went.

And wouldn't you know it? I found a penny heading out to the state highway and another one on my return walk on the same street! Wasn't that just like God to encourage me in this way? He was telling me to take a different path and He confirmed that I heard from Him. My God is that personal. He is the God of the universe, yet He still cares enough about me to walk *and* talk with me. Why He wants to is way beyond my comprehension, but I'm thankful!

To this day, I smile when I think of this particular walk. I even shared this story with my congregational leaders, who were just as encouraged as I was. We worship and love a personal God who really does want to walk and talk with us, His children.

God's Consistent Message: Walk with Me

The Spirit of God told King Asa in 2 Chronicles 15:2, "Listen to me, Asa, and all Judah and Benjamin. The LORD is with you when you are with Him. If *you seek Him*, He will be found by you, but if you forsake Him, He will forsake you," (emphasis added). Try rereading that verse, inserting your name in place of Asa's and, instead of "Judah and Benjamin," inserting the name of your community of believers.

This same concept of closeness is found on the other side of the Bible in James 4:8, "*Come near to God* and He will come near to you.*" And in 1 Thessalonians 5:16-18, "Be joyful always; *pray continually; give thanks in all circumstances*, for this is God's will for you in Christ Jesus," (emphasis added).

Our God, the One who has the power to create and take life, says He wants to walk with us. This is a key truth that sets a Bible-based faith apart from many (if not all) other religions; our God is a personal God who wants to walk with His children. The challenge in these verses is this: do we want to walk with Him?

It's been said, *"Nothing changes until something changes."* We need three things if we want to experience all of the good things that come from walking in the presence of our God. First, we must have the biblical tools necessary to screen out all the other voices screaming for our attention (including our own). Second, we must actually use these tools to *change our thinking* for a changed life to occur (Romans 12:2). Tools left lying in the toolbox are absolutely useless if we want to build on the foundation of Christ (1 Corinthians 3:10-15). And, third, we need the power of God to use those tools. Without the Spirit's power we cannot change ourselves. It is only when we say the three hardest words, "Lord, help me," that His power is released. This is the toughest of the three things.

Deciding to Walk with Your God

In the Bible, we see God acting in nature. He caused earthquakes. He turned water into wine, and dew into manna. But nature and people are different. God created humanity with a free will that He chooses not to violate. Our God, who created the entire universe, is asking us to walk with Him in a very personal way. It's His great desire for us *to want* to walk in His presence. But He will wait for us to say, "I can't do this anymore. Lord Jesus, help me to walk with You!"

If you want to personally walk in the presence of God, you must choose to think differently and surrender your will to Jesus. If not, you'll experience the same results you've always experienced. The old way of thinking just doesn't produce a changed life and Christ-like character. Does your current way of living bring you what you want in life? If it does, keep walking the same path over and over again, and you'll keep experiencing the same results. But if it doesn't, something needs to change. I've learned this truth the hard way, and have been stuck in some pretty ugly ruts until I decided I needed a change.

Take the Next Step – Trust His Directions

If you want to draw closer to Jesus, and if you want to experience the "abundant life" He came to give you, it's time to take a different road. Let the Spirit of God use the Word of God to exchange your old thinking for something new. Pick up your biblical tools to filter every message so you can listen to and follow Jesus every day everywhere.

Enjoy the journey to becoming more like Jesus. No matter how young or old you are in your faith, you can choose to walk in the presence of your God. As you walk with your God on the trails and streets He leads you down, you *will* see your own story unfold and your God *will* become very real to you.

Take the Next Step

Your journey continues with your next step.

"We are His workmanship, created in Christ Jesus unto good works, which God hath before ordained that we should walk in them." (Ephesians 2:10 KJV)

Here is one last story, about a walk I didn't take. Recently, God told me to increase my prayer time with Him, and to start my day praying about whatever He wants me to do. One morning I decided I could do this from bed, instead of going for a walk. This prayer session started off with the best of intentions, and seemed to be going well, until I looked at the clock. Then I realized that it was an hour later than when I'd started! There was no way this prayer session had gone on that long – I must have fallen asleep. I felt terrible. I felt I had robbed my God and myself, and the rest of the day was pretty rough as I got caught up in guilt.

The sad part is that I knew better. I knew all the principles I'd learned and written about in *Walk with Jesus*...and I left them here in the book! If you are like most readers, you've highlighted some important things, been touched for the moment...and then will likely leave the principles in the book and on your shelf gathering dust.

Please, don't leave what you know about Him in this book or in your head. Use your biblical tools each day to allow the Spirit to replace more of you with more of Jesus. If you're already walking with Him, keep listening to and following Jesus. If you've stopped walking or slowed down, pick up the pace!

Know this: We will never "arrive," even after we're in heaven, since Jesus will still have so much to teach us about Himself. He is an eternal God who wants us to know Him and gives us eternity to continue to deepen our relationship with Him! Each day, then, is a new walk for all of us, no matter how old we become. Old dogs can learn new tricks…as long as those dogs belong to Jesus! Walking with God will have its share of switchbacks, but remember that they're your friends. With each new challenge you'll have three choices: go back, stay still and get cold, or continue to walk toward the warmth of His love.

As you choose to walk forward you'll continue to be surprised by what you thought you knew about Jesus and yourself, and what still can be known in the future. You only know what you know at this point in time. You are God's workmanship, given the tools to walk with your God in any situation you encounter. The question is, "Will you continue to do *with* Him what He has prepared for you?"

Put on your shoes and take the next step on your journey! As you walk with your God, He will show up in some very personal and surprising ways.

"This is how we know we are in Him:
Whoever claims to live in Him
must *walk as Jesus did*."
1 John 2:5b-6

End Notes

Life is not about living, but a series of opportunities to choose an enjoyable walk with and becoming more like Jesus.

"Do your best to present yourself to God as one approved, a workman who does not need to be ashamed and who correctly handles the word of truth." (2 Timothy 2:15)

Introduction – It's time for a Walk

1. Matthew 3:16-17. An audible voice from heaven was heard by the people who attended Jesus' baptism.

2. It appears from Scripture that God, without the aid of a person, brought both Abraham (Acts 7:2-3) and Paul (Acts 9:1-9: Galatians 1:13-17) to Himself and did much of the discipling Himself as well.

3. John 21:15,19.

4. http://www.lyricsfreak.com/b/brian/where+you+go+ill+go+feat+jenn+johnson_20650277.html.

Chapter 1 – You Can Live in His Presence

1. You can purchase *More Than a Sunday Faith,* where you can read about how to use your biblical *Set Free Nowww* tools, at morethanasundayfaith.com.

2. Genesis 48:15.

3. This desire to have His people walk in His presence didn't end when the Israelites came to the Promised Land. When this tent was replaced by the Temple in Jerusalem, God filled the Temple as well (2 Chronicles 5:13-6:2).

4. You can read about how the peace offering is a tool to staying in the presence of your God at http://www.morethanasundayfaith.com/2013/07/living-each-day-in-the-peace-of-god-the-peace-offering-3/.

5. John 8:41 records that the Jewish leadership believed Jesus to be an illegitimate son. They knew who His mother was, but they couldn't be certain as to His father. In Genesis 15:2, the Spirit through Moses records Abraham calling his God by the name LORD. And it was this LORD who appeared to Abraham in Genesis 18:1.

Chapter 3 – When Your God Speaks, Are You Listening?

1. One word of caution on God speaking through people. This method can be greatly abused. Be cautious when someone says, "The Lord told me to tell you." Remember God told Israel that they were not to allow mediums to live in Israel, let alone use them to hear from God (Deuteronomy 18:10-11; Leviticus 20:6). We are to hear from God for ourselves, not rely on other people to be His voice to us. Having said that, your God will often use two or more spiritually sensitive people to confirm what He's already told you (2 Corinthians 13:1). This is important. Listen to what others are saying, but always keep listening to your Shepherd for yourself.

2. John 1:1, "In the beginning was the Word, and the Word was with God and the Word was God….Through Him all things were made." Revelation 1:2 reveals that Jesus is the Word of God. Jesus was speaking at creation. Revelation 22:20 quotes Jesus as saying, "Yes, I am coming soon." He has the first and last words in written revelation.

3. Judges 2:1-4; 10:11; 20:18ff.

4. Judges 6:4; 1 Samuel 3:6.

5. Judges 13:3.

6. 2 Samuel 2:1.

7. Some will argue there's no longer a need or possibility for God to speak directly with His children since we now have the complete written Word of God. The rationale for this belief is that the "perfect" has come, which is believed to be the Bible

(1 Corinthians 13:9). There's one problem with this thinking. 1 Corinthians 13:8 also states that when this perfect comes, knowledge "will pass away." Has knowledge ceased to increase now that we have the Bible? The answer is no. Thus, the perfect can't be the written Word of God, and the need for God's direct communication with His children still exists.

8. Loren Cunningham, *Is That Really You, God?*, YWAM Publishing.

9. You can go to www.morethasundayfaith.com to download a "Read the Bible in a Year" schedule.

Chapter 5 – A Walk Focused on Jesus

1. A more detailed discussion on how God wants a personal relationship with every believer can be found at http://www.morethanasundayfaith.com/2013/04/discipleship-copies-of-the-original-4/.

Chapter 6 – Drawing Closer

1. Leviticus 13-15 describes the unclean and clean, and their remedies.

2. Exodus 23:29-30 reveals that God said from the very start He would not wipe out every nation in one year or in one fell swoop. Joshua 2:20-22 and Judges 3:1-3 only confirm what God had promised. 2 Corinthians 12:7-10 – Jesus told Paul that He would not remove Paul's "thorn," which kept Paul humble.

Chapter 7 – Living with Jesus Everywhere

1. "The origin and meaning of the word 'church'," The Bible Pages, accessed August 6, 2013, http://www.biblepages.net/gg06.htm.

2. Acts 5:11 illustrated this truth when it states "great fear fell upon the church *and all who heard* about these events." It was people, not a building, who feared. Acts 8:1 states that "a great persecution broke out against the church at Jerusalem…and all except the apostles were scattered throughout Judea and Samaria." The Spirit points out that it was people who were scattered (not parts of any building) throughout the land of Israel.

3. "Discipleship: Copies of the Original," More Than a Sunday Faith, accessed August 6, 2013, http://www.morethanasundayfaith.com/2013/04/discipleship -copies-of-the-original-4/.

Chapter 8 - A Walk of Continual Progress

1. See chapter 16 of *More Than a Sunday Faith*, and go to www.morethanasundayfaith.com for a Bible Impact Card.

Chapter 9 – Is Your Love Cheap or Deep?

1. The Scriptures clearly teach that a child of God can never leave the presence of God (Matthew 28:20; Romans 8:38-39). We can be, however, both in and not in His presence at the same time. (Review the peek-a-boo game illustration in Chapter 1.) Yes, we are always in God's presence; and yet by turning our backs on Him, though we're in His presence, we're incapable of enjoying being in His presence. Though we are never separated, we can feel the consequences of being separated from Him.

Acknowledgements

"I thank God every time I remember you." (Philippians 1:3)

This entire journey started with the first step, encouraged by my seminary professor, Neil T. Anderson. Dr. Anderson, I want to thank you for allowing the Lord to show you how to listen to and follow Jesus using both the written and Living Word of God, and then for passing this truth on to your students.

Most of the walks described in this book took place around my own home, but there were a few that started from locations provided by loving friends and family. Meredith Harmonson, thanks for making my family part of yours and for arranging our use of the wonderful Mammoth cabin each year. Mike and Kathy Pedone, thank you for making your home available for me to gain valuable insights into ministering to future "musicianaries" through walking the streets of Tennessee. Mom, thanks for your awesome Colorado hospitality. Moran Rosenblit, thank you for making me part of your family, your friendship, and for allowing me to partner with you in the privilege of making disciples in Israel.

I also want to give a big shout out to my BIG partners. God has used you in tremendous ways to hold me accountable to the life-change process that has made my walk with and love for Jesus stronger. I greatly appreciate both you and my DHD prayer team (you all know who you are!) for being there for me through texts and emails when I needed prayer to work through an issue or fight off the enemy who didn't want this book to go beyond my computer. Thank you to the family at *New Hope Community Church*. The principles taught in this book came from our collective walk together. I praise God for you as the Spirit continues to use us to draw others closer to Jesus.

For those who know me, writing is a very difficult process. It's something the Lord has had me do while walking with Him. Having said that, I needed a lot of help from others in writing this book. To Alice Dyer, my aunt, and to Scott Mann, my very good friend, go tremendous thanks for reading and commenting on the early draft of this book. You went above and beyond the call of duty. To Merrily Versluis, my editor, you're a glutton for punishment! Thanks for graciously signing up to go through the editing process with me…again. I'm extremely grateful for your insights and suggestions that enabled me to express what I heard Jesus tell me to say. To CMA Resources, thank you for believing in this book enough to publish it.

What can I say about my awesome family? I am extremely proud of both of my children's walks with their Jesus. Douglas and DeAnna, I love you and will always be praying for you to listen to and follow Jesus everywhere you go! To Jan, my loving wife, best friend, armor bearer, and life's partner, I would not have the walk with Jesus I do without your support, love and encouragement. Thanks for taking this journey with me and for having the walk you do with Jesus. It allows both of us to not only get closer to Jesus, but also to each other.

Father, thank You for wanting to talk with me, let alone have a relationship with me. Jesus, thank You for making this relationship possible by dying and rising again for me, and also for showing me how this relationship works in the here and now by walking and talking with me every day everywhere. Spirit, thank You for bringing to me what I need to know about how to walk with Jesus, and for also providing the strength to do it.

Appendix I

Biblical Tools for Walking with Jesus

Live like you did yesterday: you'll miss walking with Jesus today and be in the same place tomorrow.

"By the grace God has given me, I laid a foundation as an expert builder, and someone else is building on it. But each one should be careful how he builds." (1 Corinthians 3:10)

One of the metaphors the Bible uses for the believer is a house (1 Corinthians 3:10-15). I live in Southern California where concrete is used as the foundation for almost every house. After laying this foundation, the construction workers will use different tools (skill saws, nail guns, measuring tapes, etc), depending on the situation, to utilize the various materials (wood, drywall, clay roofing tiles, etc) to produce a quality home.

It is the same with our walks in the presence of our God. We are not building from the ground up, though – the Spirit has a big remodeling job to do in us! Remember: Jesus didn't come to add Himself or new behaviors to us. He came to replace us with Him. When we put our faith in God, the first thing the Spirit does is to replace our old foundation with Jesus. At that point, He will use situations to tear down old sections of "our house" (Hebrews 12:1-11) and rebuild it with eternal materials.

The believer's role is to pick up and use the "tools" of biblical truths that the Spirit gives. Just like various tools have different purposes, the truths found in God's word are needed in different situations. And, just like a construction worker, we need everyday tools, along with a few specialty tools in our toolbox. Though all biblical truths are important, not all of them are necessary in every situation.

The foundational biblical tools given below (along with a few specialty tools) are the everyday tools a believer needs to replace their old way of life or "housing" with Jesus' eternal housing. Each tool is explained in greater detail in the book, *More Than a Sunday Faith.*

A Biblical Worldview: **Listen to and Follow Jesus Every Day Everywhere in Community** (John 10:27-30)

Pre-principle: Is your way of living working?
Each of us has been influenced by our education, experiences, environments, and sin nature to think and act a certain way. This is called a worldview, which colors everything we see, hear, feel, think, say and do. Any worldview other than a biblical worldview will only lead to rejection, guilt, failure, fear, and insecurity.

Specialty Tool: *Sin-confession-sin cycle.*

As believers, we turn our backs on God by choosing to live life our way. When the Spirit convicts us of our sin, we can confess it, receive forgiveness for it, and get back on our journey to walk in the presence of our God again. Yet, if we choose not to use our foundational biblical tools, we'll sin again, which leads to confession, and then eventually to sin again. I call this the sin-confession-sin cycle.

Want to stop that cycle? If so, it's time to ask, "Is my way of living working?" If not, then it's time to live with a biblical worldview, which means to listen to and follow the only One who can get you out of that cycle – Jesus.

Foundational Biblical Tools: Set Free Nowww
Secure because I'm a child of God – John 1:12; 2 Corinthians 5:17; 1 John 3:1.

We all have three basic needs: 1) to be loved ("I am

accepted"); 2) to feel safe and secure ("Life will turn out okay"); and 3) to be significant ("I can do something meaningful with my life"). The question is, where are we turning to meet those needs – Jesus or ourselves?

When a person puts their faith in Jesus, they become born again, a new creation, a child of God. We can mine this one foundational truth for a long time. We are not the same person we were before we put our faith in Jesus. We have been given a new mind – Jesus' (1 Corinthians 2:16), and a new nature – Jesus' (2 Peter 1:3-4). Therefore, we have the ability for the first time in our lives to make the right choices (Romans 6:11-14). As secure children of God, we have been given the ability to listen to and follow Jesus, who is the only One who can meet our needs. Our house can be remodeled (Appendix II)!

Specialty Tool: *Everyone has a drug of choice.* (1 John 1:8)

Each believer has what I call a "drug of choice." All believers have areas that need to be replaced with Jesus, rooms that need to be remodeled. Our drugs of choice are anything or anyone we turn to other than to Jesus to solve our daily challenges. These might be to-do lists, chemical or liquid drugs, a desire to win every argument, gossip, texting/social networking, pornography, lying, etc.

We must keep in mind that all sin, no matter what it is, separates us from the source of life – Jesus, and destroys our peace, security and significance. Thus, there is no sin that is worse or better than another, though some sins have greater consequences on this earth. Since we all have weaknesses, we can be real with each other. We can give each other the room to let the Spirit remodel our houses at His pace, not ours. Because we are secure children of God, we can choose to listen to and follow Jesus instead of taking our drugs of choice.

Entertain the truth – Psalm 119:9-16; John 8:31-32; Ephesians 6:10-18.

We only know what we know when we know it, and will act according to what we know. The question is whether what we know is true or a lie. Jesus said in Matthew 12:33-35 that our outward behavior comes from what is inside us. We need a source of truth outside ourselves to filter our thoughts through. This source is the written Word of God, which can expose the lies in our thinking and give us the truths that will set us free. It gives us the ability to recognize Jesus' voice to follow Him everywhere we go.

Specialty Tool: *We become like what we focus on and what we focus on only gets bigger.* (John 16:12-15)

What we focus on will sooner or later come out in our behavior. In other words, *you don't just fall!* If we focus on the lies, we will turn our backs on Jesus. If we focus on the truth, we'll draw closer to Him. We need the Spirit of Truth to show us the truth that exposes the lies and hurts in our lives. A good method is to ask Him what areas of your life need changing. Make a list, and then ask Him to expose the lies behind those areas.

Transform your behavior by changing your thinking – Romans 12:2.

Based upon the previous foundational biblical tool, we must stop focusing on our behavior, and start focusing on the thinking behind the behavior if we want our houses remodeled. We are "transformed by the renewing of our minds," not by exchanging one behavior for another (Matthew 23:27-28).

Specialty Tool: *You don't put new paint over old.* (Matthew 15:1-20)

When painting, we scrape off the old paint before putting on the new paint, since we don't want the old paint to chip off and take the new paint with it. It's the same with life change. Jesus didn't come to add Himself or new behaviors to us, but to replace us with Him. We don't become like Jesus by adding new behaviors to cover up our old ones.

Input then output, is the order of freedom. We input specific truths from the Word of God into our brain to filter out the lies in our thinking, leaving us with the truth as the Spirit rebuilds our houses. We become more like Jesus as God changes us from the inside out, our thinking before our behavior.

Specialty Tool: *Scripturally reason through life's situations not react to them.* (James 1:5)

Biblical critical thinking is crucial in helping us choose to walk in the presence of our God. If we react to life's situations in our strength (rather than filtering them through the Word of God), we're more likely to stray from the presence of God. The following four foundational biblical tools make up the **FREE**dom process, which enables the believer to think through a situation using specific truths so they can listen to Jesus and follow Him in their everyday world.

Freeze frame every thought – 2 Corinthians 10:3-6.
Run every thought by the Spirit of truth – John 16:12-15.

A film projector shines its light on each frame for a split second in order to show a clear picture on the screen. In the same way, a believer must shine the light of God's Word on each thought in order to clearly see what's going on in any situation. The Bible states that we must "take every thought captive" to Jesus. This includes "strongholds" (our defense mechanisms), "arguments" (the justifications for what we do), and "pretensions" (the "I-problem"). We need to ask the Spirit to show us whether these thoughts (whether inside our heads or coming at us from outside) are true or lies.

Expose and exchange the lies with the truth – Ephesians 6:10-18; 1 Peter 5:8-9; Jude 9.

This is where the warfare gets really intense. Jesus calls our adversary the "father of lies" and a "murderer" in John 8:44. Our enemy will throw his darts at us, and the only thing that will extinguish those darts is the shield of faith.

Christian cliché answers rarely work in real life. Scripture is not a holy talisman, full of verses that magically make the pain or problem go away. No, we must know how to *use* Scripture in daily life. A hammer is a good tool, but if you need a saw, a hammer is not too helpful. Specific truths put out the fiery darts/lies of the enemy. We are defenseless if we don't have them in our shields. So, if we want to experience life, we must expose the lies and replace them with specific lie-fighting truths.

Specialty Tool: *Avoid empty calories!* (Hebrews 11:25)

All sin (big or small) is pleasurable…for a season. Empty calories taste good going down, but are not helpful in the long run and are called *guilty pleasures* for a reason. Our sins, or drugs of choice, are a cheap but ineffective attempt to meet our needs. They feel good at the time, but guilt and emptiness are not far behind. If we want to feel full and satisfied, we must turn to Jesus to meet our needs by *exposing the lies* in our thinking.

Specialty Tool: *Life doesn't operate in a vacuum.* (Matthew 12:43-45)

If something is removed, something will replace it. If we remove a lie, it will come back if truth is not present. This puts us back on the sin-confession-sin cycle again. As the Spirit exposes the lies, we must stand our ground against our enemy, the source of lies/empty calories (John 8:44). We need to tell him to leave, and *exchange the lies with the specific truths* the Spirit gives us as we read through the Word of God. Believers need a constant supply of these truths throughout the year, so reading the Bible in a scheduled way (i.e. a Bible reading plan) is very helpful. From the author's experience, it's been amazing how God speaks at just the right time through a reading plan.

Exercise the truth by faith Spirit empowered – Romans 6:11-14; Galatians 5:16-26; Philippians 4:8-9.

It's time to exercise that truth now that we have it. And the more we practice that truth in the Spirit's power when challenges arise, the sooner our house will be remodeled.

Specialty Tool: *Make your faith useful, not useless.* (James 2:14-26)

Acquiring Bible knowledge is not the believer's goal; life change through using it by faith is! A mature believer has the knowledge to discern good from evil *and* practices righteousness under the Spirit's control throughout their day everywhere they go (Hebrews 5:11-14; Ephesians 5:18). If we only store up biblical knowledge, but don't use it, Scripture can make us callous to Jesus' voice. If we listen to and follow Jesus, our lives will be changed and we will be blessed in what we do (Psalm 1; James 1:22-25).

*N*ever *give up on yourself, Jesus won't* – 1 John 2:1; 1 Peter 1:15-17; Hebrews 12:2.

Our Father knows that it *takes time to retrain our brain.* His mercy covers our sin; and His grace gives us the ability to get up and walk in His presence again. He gives us another chance for victory the next time we face that challenge.

Specialty Tool: *There are do-overs, so fail forward.*

Don't waste time beating yourself up! It's our goal to walk with Jesus and never fall. But if we do, we must understand that Jesus paid for *all* our mistakes. Learn from those falls in order to not repeat them. *Learn to fail forward!*

Specialty Tool: *Do quick down – quick up exercises.*

Because we are secure children of God, our God will never give up on us, which means we can do *quick down – quick up* exercises. If you fall, don't waste time on the ground. Quickly get up and start walking in the presence of your God again. Use your **FREE**dom process to filter what you were thinking and/or feeling at the time you fell. "What lie was I holding onto? Is there a specific lie-fighting truth for this moment? Do I have and know how to use the right specialty tool(s) for this challenge?" Ask for and then put those new truths into your filter and exercise them by faith the next time you face a similar challenge with the Spirit's power.

*O*ffer *and get forgiveness constantly* – Matthew 6:14-15; 18:21-35; 2 Corinthians 2:10-11.

Specialty Tool: *Jesus is approachable!* (1 John 1:9; 2:1)

Our goal is to stay in the presence of our God. Yet, don't run away from Jesus if you sin/fall by taking your drug of choice, run toward Him! He's approachable. Don't waste time on the ground. Jesus is there with an open hand, not a fist, to help you up. We confess our sin to Jesus by telling Him and ourselves the truth. "I sinned. I see the lie I acted upon, believe it is a lie, and call it a lie." Then we ask for Jesus' forgiveness, which He gives, 100% of the time, to those who ask!

Specialty Tool: *No head time allowed!* (Romans 8:1)

Our enemy has specific tools as well, and loves to use them in our lives. One is called guilt. Once we're forgiven, though, there is no need for guilt. There is no longer any condemnation for those in Christ! When guilt tries to enter your brain over something that's already been forgiven, don't let it in. Put up your shield of faith, saying, "I've been forgiven for that." Then deny it any "head time" by thinking about something true. Don't give guilt any space – it only leads to falling again.

Specialty Tool: *Take inventory.* (Matthew 5:21-24; Romans 12:17-19)

Ask the Spirit, "Is there anything (past or present failures/sin) blocking my relationship with Jesus? If so, use your *Specialty Tool: Jesus is approachable.* Get it forgiven…right now.

Also, ask the Spirit, "Is there anyone who has hurt me that I haven't forgiven?" If so, it's time to forgive them, whether they recognize (or admit) they hurt you, or not. Forgiveness is in your best interest since it brings healing in your life.

Lastly, ask the Spirit, "Is there anyone I've hurt?" If so, it's time to ask for their forgiveness. You can be used by Jesus to draw them closer to Him.

The pain caused by our failures and/or by others can keep us in the sin-confession-sin cycle. Don't let Satan keep you down, or get a toehold in your life. Learn how forgiving God's way is all about your freedom! (See Chapter 11, *Forgiveness Keeps Your Filter Unclogged,* in *More Than a Sunday Faith,* to learn how to biblically forgive.)

When I realize that I am weak, He can be strong for me – Matthew 6:13; 26:41; 1 Pet. 5:8-9.

When you realize you're weak and want to fall – BE ALERT!! Jesus said to watch and pray so we won't enter temptation.

Being alert includes avoiding tempting situations, since our enemy is always looking for ways to trip us up. There is an exercise on pages 196-197 in *More Than a Sunday Faith* to help you discern the days, time, and places where you are most vulnerable.

Specialty Tool: *Being weak = Being strong!* (2 Corinthians 12:10)

Once you realize where and when you're vulnerable, you can call out for help from the Spirit and from fellow believers to give you the strength to become and stay free. Calling out for help is a sign of strength, not weakness.

Walk with the Spirit – Zechariah 4:6; Galatians 5:16-26; Ephesians 5:18.

The words, "Lord, help me," are some of the strongest words we can say. As we surrender our wills to the Spirit and ask Him to give us the power to exercise the truth, our lives can be changed.

Specialty Tool: *Jesus lead me, Spirit empower me.*

The more dependent upon Jesus and the Spirit we are the more independent we become. The more we ask for the Spirit to empower us, the more He takes control. And the greater control He has, the more dependent upon Him we become for every decision. The result is true independence from sin and destructive behaviors.

Walk with other believers – 1 Corinthians 10:13; Philippians 2:12 ("you" is plural); Hebrews 10:25.

Sometimes the Spirit will give us victory all by Himself, while in other situations He will use other believers to help us. To underscore this point, Jesus had more than 38 "one another" phrases written into Scripture to show us that He will use other believers in the remodeling process. The Bible reveals that we all face similar challenges. The enemy tries to convince us that our victories and failures will be unique to us. He uses this as a tool to shame us into thinking our journeys in the presence of our God are isolated from other believers. *This is a lie!*

Specialty Tool: *Get rid of the, "Yeah, but...."* (Galatians 6:2)

Yeah that's true, but.... You could probably fill in a long list of the reasons why you can't or shouldn't be vulnerable with a fellow believer in Christ. All those reasons have one thing in common: keeping you in control. This means you'll stay dependent upon your drug of choice, rather than upon the Spirit, who uses other believers as crucial remodeling tools.

Specialty Tool: *Be in a Bible Impact Group.* (James 5:16)

Jesus knows we can't be vulnerable with every believer. We can, however, be real with one or two people of the same gender. We can confess our sin, acknowledge our failures, and expose our thinking processes to another believer so they can pray for us to be healed and set free from our drugs of choice.

This is why being in a *Bible Impact Group* (BIG) is so important. It is not an accountability-to-stop-sinning group. It's a group of two-to-three people of the same gender meeting one hour per week holding each other accountable to the process of life change.

As we listen to each other talk about what area(s) of our lives the Spirit wants to remodel, we don't offer advice or counsel from our own point of view. Instead, we filter what is said by using the *Set Free Nowww* foundational biblical tools. We can be Jesus' ears and mouth to help them see the lie(s) in their thinking and answer it with truth. And while doing this, we're reinforcing those same principles in our own lives.

You can download a BIG card or order a bunch of them at www.morethanasundayfaith.com or www.CMAresources.org and start walking with and becoming more like Jesus today!

Appendix II

Your New Identity in Christ

"How great is the love the Father has lavished on us, that we should be called children of God! And that is what we are!" (1 John 3:1)

Discover for yourself what the Bible has to say about those who put their faith in Jesus.

I belong, am loved and accepted:

John 15:15 –

1 Corinthians 6:17 –

1 Corinthians 6:19, 20 –

Ephesians 1:1 –

Ephesians 1:5 –

Ephesians 2:18 –

Colossians 1:14 –

Colossians 2:10 –

I am significant:

John 15.16

Acts 1:8 –

2 Corinthians 5:17f –

Ephesians 2:6 –

Ephesians 2:10 –

Ephesians 3:12 –

Philippians 4:13 –

I am safe and secure:

Romans 8:1-2 –

Romans 8:28 –

Romans 8:35f –

2 Corinthians 1:21, 22 –

Colossians 3:3 –

Philippians 1:6 –

1 John 5:18 –

Your Identity in Christ:

Truth:

Don't waste time *discovering* who you are; instead *act* on who your Father tells you who you are.

Your identity is not based upon what you do, but upon what *Jesus* did for you.

You *are* a saint with a sin challenge.

You've been given a new mind – Christ's – so you can *think* correctly.

You've been given a new nature – Christ's – so you can *act* correctly.

The question is, will you *choose* to exercise the truth by faith Spirit empowered in your everyday situations?

ABOUT THE AUTHOR

Chris Suitt has walked with and been in the process of becoming more like Jesus for over 40 years, been married to his wife, Jan, for over 27 years, and is the father of two adult children. He also pastors, makes disciples and trains others to make disciples around the world through *Church Multiplication Associates*, *the eXtreme Tour*, and *Hope for Israel*. He is the author of *More Than a Sunday Faith* and various articles published online.

PASS ALONG THE TOOLS

If the Lord has used *Walk with Jesus* in your life, you can pass on that blessing in three ways. One, tell a friend about how the Lord drew you closer to Him because you applied the principles in this book. Two, purchase a copy of *Walk with Jesus* and give it to the person the Lord lays on your heart. And three, go to www.morethanasundayfaith.com and make a donation that allows the author to make copies available to those who can't afford them.

www.ingramcontent.com/pod-product-compliance
Lightning Source LLC
LaVergne TN
LVHW021349080426

835508LV00020B/2178